Linguistic Lar _large_ pes

MULTILINGUAL MATTERS SERIES
**Series Editor:** Professor John Edwards,
*St. Francis Xavier University, Antigonish, Nova Scotia, Canada*

**Other Books in the Series**

For more details of these or any other of our publications, please contact:
Multilingual Matters, Frankfurt Lodge, Clevedon Hall,
Victoria Road, Clevedon, BS21 7HH, England
http://www.multilingual-matters.com

**MULTILINGUAL MATTERS 136**
*Series Editor*: John Edwards

# Linguistic Landscapes
## A Comparative Study of Urban Multilingualism in Tokyo

Peter Backhaus

**MULTILINGUAL MATTERS LTD**
Clevedon • Buffalo • Toronto

**Library of Congress Cataloging in Publication Data**
Backhaus, Peter
Linguistic Landscapes: Comparative Study of Urban Multilingualism in Tokyo /
Peter Backhaus.
Multilingual Matters: 136
Includes bibliographical references and index.
1. Multilingualism. 2. Signs and symbols. 3. Multilingualism–Japan–Tokyo. I. Title.
P115.B32 2007
404'.2–dc22          2006031787

**British Library Cataloguing in Publication Data**
A catalogue entry for this book is available from the British Library.

EAN-13: 978-1-85359-947-7 (hbk)
EAN-13: 978-1-85359-946-0 (pbk)

**Multilingual Matters Ltd**
*UK*: Frankfurt Lodge, Clevedon Hall, Victoria Road, Clevedon BS21 7HH.
*USA*: UTP, 2250 Military Road, Tonawanda, NY 14150, USA.
*Canada*: UTP, 5201 Dufferin Street, North York, Ontario M3H 5T8, Canada.

The policy of Multilingual Matters/Channel View Publications is to use papers that
are natural, renewable and recyclable products, made from wood grown in
sustainable forests. In the manufacturing process of our books, and to further support
our policy, preference is given to printers that have FSC and PEFC Chain of Custody
accreditation. The FSC and/or PEFC logos will appear on those books where full
accreditation has been granted to the printer concerned.

Typeset by Florence Production Ltd.
Printed and bound in Great Britain by MPG Books Ltd.

306.44 BAC

06000875X

# Contents

# Acknowledgements

This book would never have made its way to the printing press without the help of a great many people. First of all, I want to express my gratitude to Florian Coulmas (German Institute for Japanese Studies, Tokyo) for his invaluable support from the first word to the last and throughout the years it took to write them all. Just to keep things short here: I couldn't have had a better supervisor, in whatever respect.

I am further indebted to Ulrich Ammon, my co-supervisor at the University of Duisburg-Essen, for his helpful comments and the incredibly flexible organisation of his schedule. In addition, I have been fortunate enough to be in regular contact with Masato Yoneda (National Institute for Japanese Language) and Fumio Inoue (Meikai University), whose advice more than once saved me from losing my way in the streets of Tokyo. Their enthusiasm has been a great encouragement for me, and it still is.

A large part of this book was prepared in the course of a research project funded by the German Research Foundation (DFG) between 2002 and 2004. It was hosted at the University of Duisburg-Essen's Institute of East Asian Studies. My empirical research in Tokyo was made possible by a seven-month scholarship from the German Institute for Japanese Studies (DIJ) in 2004/2005. In addition, the National Institute for Japanese Language and the Tokyo University of Foreign Studies were kind enough to receive me as a guest researcher for several months in 2003 and 2004, respectively. I would like to express my sincere gratitude to all the people and organisations involved, not only for their generous financial support.

Many other people in some way or other have contributed to the making of this book. I am particularly grateful to M. Barni (Siena), H.-J. Chen (Berlin), L. Du (Duisburg), G. Extra and K. Yağmur (Tilburg), D. Gorter (Amsterdam), P. Heinrich (always on the move) and all my colleagues in Duisburg, J. Hibiya (Tokyo), E. Holenstein (Tokyo), T. Kawahara, S. Miyoshi, S. Tanaka and everyone at the JACET Study Group on Language Policy, M. Kim (Osaka), J.S. Lee (Dearborn), D. Long (Tokyo), J.C. Maher (Tokyo), H. Oda and K. Yamashiro (Tokyo), H. Shōji

(Osaka), N. Tennant and C. Lowe (King's Cross), M. Urano (Tokyo), M.-H. Yang (Tokyo), and K.-S. Ziemer (Setterich).

My special thanks go to Bernard Spolsky, who (among other things) provided the foreword to this book; John Edwards, who supervised the revision of the manuscript and came up with a decent title; as well as Tommi and Marjukka Grover at Multilingual Matters, to whom I must have been one of their more complicated cases.

When I started my research in Tokyo in spring 2003, my first child had just been born. The second followed when I was finishing the main parts of the data analysis in April 2004. The coming of our latest family member now roughly coincides with the submission of the final version of the manuscript. I know that much of the time spent on writing this book should have gone somewhere else. My apologies and deepest gratitude to Yuri, Mio, Lina, and, most of all, Shin.

Tokyo, June 2006

# Foreword by Bernard Spolsky

Over the past 30 years or so, a number of scholars have been excited to discover or rediscover the riches revealed by a casual or systematic investigation of urban public signs. Somewhat inappropriately labelled 'linguistic landscape', there are signs even of a developing sub-field of sociolinguistics or language policy. Essentially, the topic of interest is the choice of language in public signs in urban space (which is why 'cityscape' might be a preferable term).

The term 'linguistic landscape' appears to have been first used by Landry and Bourhis in a paper they published in 1997 (Landry & Bourhis, 1997) reporting on the perceptions of francophone high school students of the language of public signs in Canadian provinces. It was applied by Ben-Rafael and Shohamy (Ben-Rafael *et al.*, 2001) to describe their counts of signs in various Israeli communities. But, as the excellent review in Chapter 3 of this book shows, the topic has a much longer history. In a study of the spread of English published in 1977, Rosenbaum and his colleagues (Rosenbaum *et al.*, 1977) include counts of the relative numbers of English and Hebrew signs found in a Jerusalem street. My own interest dates from a visit to Jerusalem in 1979: it became a technique for studies of vernacular literacy in various parts of the world, and the basis of a chapter in the description of the languages of the Old City of Jerusalem that Cooper and I published (Spolsky & Cooper, 1983, 1991).

A number of interesting articles and reports of studies are scattered in various journals and collections (including a recent special issue of *The International Journal of Multilingualism*; see Gorter, 2006), but, until now, there has been no serious attempt to define the field and to investigate its problematic methodologies. This is why I find Backhaus's book so refreshing and significant.

Against the background of a review of earlier work, he tackles the critical methodological issues. Attracted by the seeming objectivity of quantitative studies in the social sciences, it is not unreasonable to want to count signs and classify them by language and function. The first problem, as Backhaus makes clear, is deciding what counts as a sign. Some are easy: street names (although our own study of the Old City of Jerusalem was held up until we realised that some of the signs were in fact two signs placed one on top of the other), advertising posters and graffiti are commonly framed and so countable – but how do you deal with the multilingualism of some shop signs or the complexity of signs in a shop window? Backhaus considers this problem carefully, and the equally challenging problem of determining where to carry out his investigation. Downtown areas, it seems, can vary in their preferred languages (how else do you recognise Chinatown in an American city?), so that incautious selection of streets to be observed can lead to misleading results. And interpretation of language choices must take into account the state of literacy: only a comparatively small set of India's many languages occur on public signs, and in much of the world, vernacular literacy lags behind standard language literacy. Thus, what is sometimes interpreted as differences in language choice may well be the result of a difference in literacy development.

His own study starts only when he has made decisions on these critical methodological issues. He then provides a detailed case study of Tokyo, a city that the naive foreigner dazzled by the striking (and often electronic) display of three Japanese script types in public signs at first assumes to be as monolingual as the huge crowds that threaten to overwhelm him as he emerges from an underground. It turns out of course that, just as in many other large international cities, public signs reveal a complex but significant pattern of language choice. In Tokyo, Backhaus also reveals the evidence that the language of some signs is 'managed' – the result of explicit decisions of central and local government agencies – rather than the result of choices of the sign owner or maker. In this way, he makes an important step to fit public signs into the study of language management.

This book is not the first study of public signs in urban space, but one of the first to tackle this significant topic with the kind of self-consciousness that promises an advance of understanding of a complex field. It presents a rigorous and cautiously designed empirical study of a single city while raising perceptively the technical and theoretical questions that will need to be resolved to permit safe generalisations. It may well turn out that studying public signs is simply an attractive technique for investigating one aspect of sociolinguistic ecology. Or, with continuing intelligent application and interpretation, it could well develop into a solid theory of the use of language in public visual space. In any case, this volume by Backhaus provides a very necessary basis for future research in the area.

# Chapter 1
# *Introduction*

The city is a place of language contact. City walls throughout human history have attracted people of various origins with differing linguistic backgrounds. This applies to ancient capitals like Rome, Athens, or Constantinople just as it holds for post-modern metropolises like New York, London, Paris, or Tokyo. The spatial coexistence of different languages and linguistic varieties has made the city a favourable environment for variationist studies (e.g. Labov, 1972; Milroy, 1980; Trudgill, 1974) and, more recently, multilingualism research (e.g. Extra & Yağmur, 2004; García & Fishman, 1997; Mackey, 2000). The bulk of this research has focused on spoken language, whereas written language has not been given much attention so far. The city, however, is not only 'a place of talk', as Halliday (1978: 154) has emphasised. It is a place of writing and reading, too.

This study focuses on urban language contact in the written medium: the languages of the signs. Every urban environment is a myriad of written messages on public display: office and shop signs, billboards and neon advertisements, traffic signs, topographic information and area maps, emergency guidance and political poster campaigns, stone inscriptions, and enigmatic graffiti discourse. These messages bring together a variety of languages and scripts, the total of which constitutes the linguistic landscape of a place. The aim of this book is to provide a first general introduction to the study of language on signs and show what insights about multilingualism and language contact can be gained from this type of research.

The book consists of three shorter and two longer chapters alternating in order. Chapter 2 is a brief theoretical introduction to language on signs. It explores the semiotic properties of this special type of language use distinct from most other forms of written and spoken communication. The visibility and salience of these messages makes up the linguistic landscape, a term that is only gradually gaining currency in multilingualism research. Chapter 2 reviews the common definitions of the term and introduces a terminological distinction between the process and the results of linguistic landscape actions. It closes with a few comments about the heuristic potential of linguistic landscape research in the study of multi-lingualism.

Chapter 3 gives an overview of previous approaches to language on signs in various places around the world. The review spans from the pioneer research of the 1960s and 1970s to an accumulation of linguistic landscape approaches since the turn of the century. Included are studies from comparatively monolingual, traditionally bilingual, and highly multilingual environments in North America, Europe, Africa, and Asia. In part due to the fact that many of them have been available only in languages other than English, most previous studies do not directly refer to each other. Nevertheless it will be seen that there are many common points, despite differing research environments and research interests.

Chapter 4 establishes the link between the theoretical and the empir-ical part of this book. It summarises the basic points made in previous research and presents some general conclusions. This is done by intro-ducing an overall framework for the study of the linguistic landscape. The framework is based on three guiding questions that can be found underlying all previous approaches to language on signs. They refer to the sign writers, the sign readers, and the dynamics of the language contact situation as a whole, respectively:

(1) Linguistic landscaping by whom?
(2) Linguistic landscaping for whom?
(3) Linguistic landscape *quo vadis*?

Chapter 4 also touches on some methodological issues of empirical research into language on signs. Discussing the main problems with regard to survey areas, survey items, and linguistic categorisation, it emphasises the importance of a sound methodology of data collection for this type of research.

Chapter 5 applies the framework introduced in Chapter 4 in practice. It works with a sample of 2444 multilingual signs collected in spring 2003 in the centre of Tokyo. The data are discussed on the basis of the following nine analytical categories: languages contained; combination patterns; differences between official and non-official signs; regularities in geographic distribution; availability of translation or transliteration; order of the languages combined; visibility of the multilingual nature of a sign; occurrence of linguistic idiosyncrasies; and coexistence of older and newer versions of a given type of sign.

A closer analysis of the data will bring to light various insights about Tokyo's linguistic landscape and the points referred to in the three guiding questions: the writers of multilingual signs, their readers, and the languages and scripts in contact. They are summarised in Chapter 6, which draws some general conclusions about the city's linguistic landscape. It emphasises that the study of language on signs is a promising new research field that may provide valuable insights about multilingualism and language contact, both in Tokyo and elsewhere.

Linguistic landscape research is a relatively young sociolinguistic subdiscipline for which few theoretical preliminaries have been developed so far. Since some of the relevant literature was not yet available when I conducted my empirical research in Tokyo, the order of the parts of this book does not completely faithfully represent the order in which these parts have actually been prepared. This becomes most obvious from the fact that some of the surveys discussed as 'previous' approaches in Chapter 3 have actually been published after the 2003 Tokyo survey. Nevertheless, it was considered necessary to include them into this first overview of linguistic landscape research because they are substantial to the development of the discipline worldwide.

Before entering the main part, a few general remarks about terminology and notation should be made. Though the second half of the book focuses on Japan, care has been taken that the discussion remains accessible also without knowledge of Japanese. Technical terms about the Japanese writing system have been kept to a minimum. They are explained at the beginning of section 3.10, which discusses previous linguistic landscape research in Tokyo. A closer account of the Japanese language is given in Shibatani (1990) and Tsujimura (1996). More about the Japanese writing system and its development can be found in Gottlieb (1995), Seeley (1991), Stalph (1996), and Twine (1991).

All translations are attached in square brackets. Japanese terms mentioned in running text are transliterated according to the rules of the Hepburn system (SWET, 1989). They are indicated by italics and – where necessary – attached in their original script in summarising tables. Transliterations cited from signs are not marked by italics but given in quotes. An example is the toponym *shinbashi*, which may be encountered on official signs alternately as 'Shinbashi' or 'Shimbashi'. I follow notational conventions in using slashes to enclose phonemes and in indicating single graphemes by angled brackets. An example is Japanese syllabic /n/, which is represented in the Roman alphabet as <n> but can be altered into <m> when preceding <m>, <b>, or <p>.

Where directly quoting Roman alphabet texts from signs I make no effort to imitate the original design with regard to line make-up, font type, font size, etc. However, I do follow the original in the use and non-use of capital letters.

# Chapter 2
# *Semiotic Background and Terminology*

This chapter gives an introduction to the basic characteristics of language use on signs. Exploring the semiotic background to written language in public space, it will be held that language on signs is a specific type of language use distinct from most other forms of written and spoken communication in everyday life. The visibility and salience of language on signs constitutes what has now come to be referred to as the linguistic landscape of a place. The term will be discussed in more detail by reviewing some of its recent definitions. It will be held that the study object of linguistic landscape research should be confined to language on signs, since an expansion to other forms of language use in the public sphere would water down the usefulness of the concept as a whole. In addition, a terminological distinction between linguistic landscape and linguistic landscaping will be made.

## 2.1 Signs

The noun 'sign', according to the *Oxford Dictionary of English*, has the following five meanings (Soanes & Stevenson, 2003: 1645):

1 an object, quality, or event whose presence indicates the probable presence or occurrence of something else . . .
2 a gesture or action used to convey information or instruction . . . a gesture used in a system of sign language
3 a notice on public display that gives information or instruction in a written or symbolic form
4 (also zodiacal sign) *Astrology* each of the twelve equal sections into which the zodiac is divided . . .
5 *Mathematics* the positiveness or negativeness of a quantity.

Two of these entries, 1 and 3, are of importance to the present study. First of all, it is common knowledge that 'sign' is a key term in semiotics. The semiotic sign comprises any meaningful unit interpreted as standing for something other than itself. This type of meaning is included in entry 1. Signs usually take a physical form, such as sounds, images, acts, etc. From a semiotic point of view, the world we live in is a world of signs. Anything we understand about ourselves and what is happening around us is based on emitting and interpreting signs. Communication in whatever way without them would be inconceivable.

Best known in semiotic theory are two conceptions of the sign. One is based on the theoretical framework of the Swiss linguist Ferdinand de Saussure (1857–1913); the other follows the US American philosopher Charles S. Peirce (1839–1914). According to Saussurean semiology, the basic characteristic of the sign is a bilateral relationship between a 'signifier' as its material form, and a 'signified' as its conceptual content (Saussure, 1916: 65–70). Most adherents of Peirce, who has assumed a triadic interaction between a signifying 'representamen', a conceptual 'interpretant', and a designated 'object', emphasise the interpretation process and the role of an interpreting entity (hearer, reader, etc.) in making sense of a given sign. This 'pragmatic' dimension of the sign is not captured by Saussure's dyadic conception (Chandler, 2002: 32–6).

A second meaning of the term 'sign' relevant to this study is referred to in entry 3 of the above quotation: that of an inscribed surface displayed in public space in order to convey a message of wider concern to a non-specified group of readers. This type of sign is used in order to disseminate messages of general public interest, such as topographic information, directions, warnings, etc. Public signs also appear in commercial contexts like marketing and advertising, where their function is to draw attention to a business or product. There is no clear-cut distinction between commercial and non-commercial signs though, because the former can provide information of general interest, too. The semantic differences between the two types of signs given in entries 1 and 3 are fundamental enough to allow for a clear understanding about which one is referred to from context. Where it is necessary to explicitly distinguish between the two, I will use the term 'semiotic sign' as opposed to 'public sign'.

Public signs are a specific type of semiotic sign in that they too stand for something other than themselves. Take as an example the name of a company attached to the front of a building. The sign on which the name is inscribed indicates that the premises of the company are situated in this building. The sign represents the company as a whole. The meaning to be conferred – 'This is the building of company X' – arises out of the combination of the sign with its referent, the building to which it is attached. In this sense, a public sign is in itself a signifier that relates to a specific signified, such as a company, a product, a place, a rule, or some other concept. A sign need not necessarily be attached to its referent though. Instead, it can give a direction how to get there, as in the case of guidance signs, or simply call attention to it, as advertisement signs do.

From a semiotic point of view, a public sign makes sense only in combination with its referent. The sign of company X does not fulfil its designating function properly on the sign writer's desk or when attached to the building of company Y. It has to be put up at the right point in time and space. This applies not only to signs designating material objects, but to all other types of public messages, too. Joseph *et al.* give the following example:

> A flat metal disc of characteristic size and design bearing certain Arabic numerals and attached to a pole planted by the roadside may be called a speed-limit sign. And in this usage it may count as a 'sign' from the moment of manufacture until long after it has been uprooted and consigned to a rubbish tip. But this usage is of no interest to the semiologist, who is concerned with the object only in so far as it functions semiotically, *as* a sign. And it can function as a sign only when *in situ*, i.e. when located in the appropriate topographical context. (2001: 209, emphasis original)

Following Peircean theory, the authors also underline the necessity of an interpreting entity. Unless interpreted by someone, human being or other, a public sign has no meaning (see Keller (1995: 119) for a counter-perspective). As Joseph *et al.* further explain:

> Even when located in an appropriate environment, an object functions semiotically only in so far as someone makes it do so. The signhood of the speed-limit sign is not immanent in it. However impeccably positioned, it is not a sign when nobody is around to see it, for instance. Or when seen by strangers to our civilization who have no idea what to make of it. Signhood is conferred on a sign – on what thereby becomes a sign – if and when human beings (or semiotically competent creatures) attach a signification to it that goes beyond its intrinsic physical properties, whether in furtherance of a particular programme of activities, or to link different aspects or phases of their activities, to enrich their understanding of their local circumstances or general situation. (2001: 210, emphasis original)

More parallels between semiotic and public signs can be identified when taking a closer look at the different ways in which a sign makes sense. Following Peirce, it is generally held that a sign can function semiotically in basically three ways: as an index, as an icon, or as a symbol. An index is considered the most archaic type of sign. It is a sign with a signifier directly connected or pointing to its signified. There is a factual relationship between signifier and signified, which can be immediately observed or inferred. Commonly quoted examples are natural signs such as smoke indicating fire, medical symptoms indicating physical disease, or signals such as a knock on a door or the ringing of a phone.

A second possible way by which a relationship between signifier and signified can be established is through iconicity. In such a case the signifier is linked to its object of reference by virtue of resemblance or likeness. Examples are portraits, diagrams, or imitative gestures. The third type of sign is the symbol, for which the link between signifier and signified is arbitrary. It is based on neither similarity nor factual closeness but purely determined by convention. The most comprehensive symbolic sign system is language, which mainly functions by virtue of conventional speech signs. The three types of signs – index, icon, and symbol – are not mutually exclusive, but the relationship between the signifier and the signified of a sign can be based on more than one property (Chandler, 2002: 36–42).

Index, icon, and symbol are concepts applicable to different ways of information provision on public signs. Characteristic features of indexicality are arrows and other pointing elements used to show a direction in which the indicated object is to be found. These signs function by virtue of contiguity between signifier and signified. Use of iconic elements is a frequent strategy on public signs, too. They appear in the form of pictograms – standardised pictorial marks containing messages of an informative or directive nature without relying on a specific language (Kjørup, 2004). Another frequent example of iconic elements on public signs is maps, which provide geographic information through a complex graphic replication of the surrounding area. Symbolic elements on public signs refer to all forms of information provision by means of written language, which will be discussed in more detail in the next section.

Indexicality is often understood as the general context-dependency of all types of signs, including public signs. As Scollon and Scollon hold:

> All signs, whether they are icons or symbols are also indexes. That is because all signs must be located in the material world to exist. Information and knowledge must be represented by a system of signs – icons, symbols, and indexes; information and knowledge cannot have independent existence. The familiar stop sign on the street corner is a symbol in several ways: The letters 'S', 'T', 'O', and 'P' symbolize the English word 'stop' which itself symbolizes the meaning 'to progress no further'. It also symbolizes this meaning through the conventional use of a red color on a hexagonal background. Until it is placed in the world, this sign only means to stop in the abstract. On the sign painter's bench it does not mean that he should stop painting. It only means that a car should stop when it is placed physically in the world at a place such as a street intersection. This shift from abstract meaning potential to actual, real-world meaning is the property of indexicality. The sign abstractly symbolizes 'to stop', but indexes where and how and who in what

container is to stop in the real world only when it is grounded in the material world of cement roadways, curbs, and metal poles. (2003: vii–viii; see also 3.7)

According to Scollon and Scollon, the necessity of a public sign to be set up in its appropriate place in the material world in order to function properly is a problem of indexicality. With regard to the distinction between index, icon, and symbol, two levels need to be kept apart. One is the semiotic mode chosen to convey a message, for instance by means of written language (symbolic), pictograms (iconic), or arrows (indexical). On a higher level, each message to be conveyed is context-dependent and directly related to the spatial circumstances of its use. In this sense, indexicality is a property of all signs.

## 2.2 Language on Signs

Language is a symbolic sign system in which conventional speech signs (morphemes, words, sentences, etc.) represent meanings. Used on public signs, language comes in its written form. This way of representation differs from spoken language in various respects. In using visual rather than acoustic speech signs, writing escapes the evanescence of the spoken word. Written language is permanent. It is not bound to the immediate time of utterance but can exist independently of it (Coulmas, 2003: 11; Günther & Pompino-Marschall, 1996: 907). Being dissolvable from the circumstances of its production, written language lends itself far more easily than spoken language to transmitting information to an unspecified group of people in public space.

In a typology suggested by Wienold (1994) language use on signs is characterised as part of one distinguishable type of language use in everyday life. Referred to by Wienold as 'inscriptions', this type is defined as:

> written uses of language which do not have a recognizable emitter and are not meant for special receivers. They can be read/received by anyone coming into appropriate distance. They do not arise out of or establish or promote personal relationships and are not interpreted that way (as conversation is). (1994: 640)

Wienold (1994, 1995) includes in this type of language use instances of inscriptions that would not normally be regarded as public signs in the sense defined above, for instance language on clothes, electric appliances, and other everyday commodities. Nevertheless his suggested definition captures the basic characteristics of language on signs, which are lack of a recognisable emitter and lack of a specified target group. Even if a sign does contain information about its originator, this originator is usually an indistinct larger entity – a private or official organisation – rather than an individual person (see also Harweg, 1979: 10). The sign reader has no immediate means of responding to the transmitted message because the originator of the message is absent. The latter, on the other hand, has to be aware of the fact that they deal with a completely unknown readership. Access to a sign is free to everyone in sight. It cannot be restricted by the issuing authority in any reasonable way.

These are properties that distinguish language on signs from virtually all forms of spoken language, an exception being pre-recorded announcements at public facilities such as stations and airports, which share many of the characteristics of inscriptions (Wienold, 1994: 647). Due to its indexical qualities, language on signs also differs from various other forms of written language use. Personal letters, diaries, books, or newspapers do not require to be read at a certain point in space in order to make sense. Functioning independently of their emplacement, they are clearly distinct from language used on signs. This is of relevance with regard to the definition of the term 'linguistic landscape', to which we will turn next.

## 2.3 The Linguistic Landscape

According to the commonly quoted definition by Landry and Bourhis (1997: 23) the linguistic landscape refers to 'the visibility and salience of languages on public and commercial signs in a given territory or region'. More precisely:

> The language of public road signs, advertising billboards, street names, place names, commercial shop signs, and public signs on government buildings combines to form the linguistic landscape of a given territory, region, or urban agglomeration. (Landry & Bourhis, 1997: 25)

Landry and Bourhis's definition makes it clear that the study object of linguistic landscape research is language on signs in public space. This point has been re-emphasised in a current state-of-the-art paper by Gorter (2006: 2), who holds that linguistic landscape research is concerned with 'the use of language in its written form in the public sphere'. Likewise, Ben-Rafael *et al.* (2006: 14) define the linguistic landscape as referring to 'any sign or announcement located outside or inside a public institution or a private business in a given geographical location.'

Another terminological suggestion has recently been made by Itagi and Singh in their introductory chapter to a publication about the linguistic landscape of India (Itagi & Singh, 2002a). They paraphrase the terms 'Linguistic Landscape/Landscaping (LL)' as 'language use in its written form (visible language) in the public sphere' (Itagi & Singh, 2002b: ix). Though directly referring to Landry and Bourhis's seminal paper of 1997, Itagi and Singh's conception of the term 'linguistic landscape' slightly deviates from the definition by Landry and Bourhis in that it includes as potential study objects items such as newspapers, visiting cards, and other print media (Itagi & Singh, 2002b: ix). Towards the end of their paper the authors go one step further even in arguing that 'LL need not and should not be construed as having a bias towards written language' (Itagi & Singh, 2002b: xi). It is obvious that this 'broader view of LL' would necessarily involve an expansion of the subject matter of linguistic landscape research far beyond the initial definition by Landry and Bourhis.

With regard to future research, the question of what the term 'linguistic landscape' should and should not encompass evidently is of crucial importance. The point of view taken in this book is as follows: due to the distinctive semiotic features of language on signs as explored in the previous section, it is reasonable to stick to the definition formulated by Landry and Bourhis rather than to expand the term to a hardly definable variety of other arenas of language use in the public sphere. The present study therefore will deal with language on signs only.

Itagi and Singh's above-quoted usage of the two terms 'linguistic landscape' and 'linguistic landscaping', both abbreviated as 'LL', implies a potentially useful terminological distinction. Though no direct explanation about the difference between the two is given, their use throughout Itagi and Singh (2002a) suggests that the term in its gerund form refers to the planning and implementation of actions pertaining to language on signs (e.g. Singh, 2002), whereas the noun denotes the result of these actions (e.g. Mohan, 2002). Use of the two terms in the present book will be based on this distinction.

In closing this chapter, a few general comments about the heuristic potential of linguistic landscape research should be made. Reh (2004: 38; see 3.6) has emphasised that the study of language on signs 'enables conclusions to be drawn regarding, among other factors, the social layering of the community, the relative status of the various societal segments, and the dominant cultural ideals.' Similarly, Ben-Rafael *et al.* (2006: 27; see 3.3) underscore that 'LL analysis allows us to point out patterns representing different ways in which people, groups, associations, institutions and government agencies cope with the game of symbols within a complex reality.' These qualities of the linguistic landscape make it a useful and still vastly underexplored research tool for the study of multilingualism, which deserves to be given closer attention in the years to come.

The present study is intended to contribute to this development. It aims to show that the study of language on signs can provide valuable insights into the linguistic situation of a given place, including common patterns of language and script use, official language policies, prevalent language attitudes, power relations between different linguistic groups, and the long-term consequences of language and script contact, among others.

## Chapter 3

# *Previous Approaches to the Linguistic Landscape: An Overview*

The term 'linguistic landscape' has only relatively recently come into use in English literature on the topic. Lack of a summarising term has had the unfavourable effect that previous studies more often than not have been conducted in ignorance of similar types of research that had already been done. The aim of this chapter is to give an overview of previous linguistic landscape research, explore the basic points made so far, and show how they relate to each other.

Interest in language on signs has been particularly pronounced in environments inhabited by two distinct linguistic groups. The review therefore starts with research in officially bilingual cities: Brussels (Tulp, 1978; Wenzel, 1996); Montreal, Canada (CLF, 2000; Monnier, 1989); Jerusalem (Ben-Rafael *et al.*, 2004, 2006; Rosenbaum *et al.*, 1977; Spolsky & Cooper, 1991); and two smaller cities in the Netherlands and in Spain (Cenoz & Gorter, 2006). Next follow two studies of linguistically less straightforward environments: a comparative approach to the linguistic landscapes of Paris and Dakar (Calvet, 1990, 1994) and a survey about multilingual signs in Lira, a smaller town in Uganda (Reh, 2004). After some general observations by Scollon and Scollon (2003) about language on signs worldwide, we finally turn to empirical studies in three cities dominated by one linguistic group: Rome (Bagna & Barni, 2005, 2006; Griffin, 2004); Bangkok (Huebner, 2006; Smalley, 1994); and Tokyo (Inoue, 2000; Masai, 1972; Someya, 2002; Tōshikyō, 2000).

The review also deals with methodological issues, which, even though they may appear trivial, can constitute a major obstacle to conducting empirical research into the linguistic landscape. The main theoretical and practical problems discussed will be summarised in Chapter 4.

## 3.1 Brussels: A *Coiffeur* But No *Kapper*

With a French-speaking Walloon majority and a Dutch-speaking Flemish minority Brussels is a classical example of a bilingual city. Due to the prohibition to include questions about language use in official census questionnaires, no reliable data about the proportion of Franco-phone and Flemish speakers are available. However, it is commonly assumed that Flemish is first language to about 20% of the city's total population. This low share may come as a surprise. Even though Belgium is an officially trilingual country – the third language being that of a small German-speaking minority along the Belgium–Germany border, its capital Brussels is not situated at the language border dividing the Francophone part of the country in the south from the Flemish-speaking north. The city is a bilingual island within Flemish territory, which used to be almost completely Dutch-speaking. Yet in less than two centuries Brussels turned into a predominantly Francophone metropolis. Factors triggering this Frenchification process were the influx of French-speaking population and shift patterns in favour of French, adopted by both foreign migrants and speakers of Dutch (Baetens Beardsmore, 2000; Witte & Baetens Beardsmore, 1987).

The linguistic complexity of the situation has made Brussels a favourable environment for linguistic landscape research. An early survey was conducted by Tulp (1978), who examined the languages of commercial billboards. The aim of her study was to demonstrate how language usage patterns on these signs have been contributing to the city's gradual Frenchification. Assuming that the visibility of a language in public space is vital for its perceived ethnolinguistic vitality, Tulp anticipated a point to be empirically confirmed by Landry and Bourhis (1997) several decades later.

Tulp focused on large-sized billboards, covering a space of 10 m$^2$ and more, in and around Brussels. The area selected included major tram, metro, and bus routes, which were surveyed once in August and again in December 1976. The number of items collected on both occasions amounts to over 2000. The basic quantitative findings show that French dominates the linguistic landscape. Around two-thirds of the collected items were monolingual French billboards. The residuary items were mainly monolingual Dutch. Billboards containing both languages accounted for less than 10%. Items without text or in a language other than French or Dutch also occurred, but were of minor quantitative importance (Tulp, 1978: 278).

The representative strength of the two languages shows a clear geographic tendency. The further one goes to the north, where the majority of the Flemish population is known to live, the more Dutch billboards one is likely to see. French, on the other hand, is predomi-nant in the south of Brussels and even in the officially Flemish territory that divides the city from the Walloon language border. Dutch is virtu-ally invisible in many of these regions. French billboards also dominate the areas around the major railway and metro stations of the city (Tulp, 1978: 278–9).

Tulp's overall evaluation of her findings is critical. She argues that Brussels' linguistic landscape is not bilingual but predominantly French with only 'here and there a small place for the Flemish'. She complains that this predominance of French in the streets of the Belgian capital implies to visitors and people newly moved to the area that Brussels is a by and large French-speaking city, a perception that in itself will trigger further Frenchification. In order to stop this process of language shift and secure future French–Dutch bilingualism in Brussels, Tulp demands that there be 'true' bilingualism in outward advertising. The linguistic landscape should not reflect the different demographic strengths of the two linguistic groups, but both languages must be available to equal degrees (Tulp, 1978: 284–6).

A similar survey about language on commercial signs was conducted by Wenzel (1996) more than 15 years later. Wenzel's main survey area was a 12.3 km route from the south-east to the north-west of Brussels. Also included were larger commuting roads, the three main stations (Central, North, South), and a football stadium. Like Tulp, she conducted her survey twice, once in February and again in April 1992. In total she collected 701 items for her sample, including large billboards with an approximate size of 9 m², smaller posters around 2 m², and shop signs. The latter were not part of her quantitative analysis. Apart from the overall representative strength of the languages involved, Wenzel's analysis includes the following issues: geographic distribution; order of the languages and combinations; and correlations between language and service or product offered.

The determination of the languages involved some methodological problems, especially where English product names were concerned. Wenzel (1996: 47–8) determined that English brand names were not counted as English texts. Consequently, the following examples were recorded as French and Dutch, not English:

Fiez-vous à votre première impression.
The new Rover 800 series.

Vertrouw op uw eerste indruk.
The new Rover 800 series.

Other problems evolved from language-mixing. An example is the slogan 'formidiesel', a pun created for a car advertisement. It blends the word 'diesel' with the word 'formidable' (French) or 'formidabel' (Dutch). Because in 'formidiesel' the slight orthographic difference between French and Dutch gets lost, a clear determination of the language becomes impossible. In general, however, such blends of French and Dutch were the exception rather than the rule on commercial signs in Brussels (Wenzel, 1996: 47–8).

The basic quantitative results of Wenzel's survey are given in Table 3.1. In her sample, 56.5% of the billboards were in French, 24.2% in Dutch, 9.7% in English, and 7.1% without text. The residuary 2.5% were bilingual in French and Dutch, French and English, or Dutch and English. Comparing these figures to Tulp's findings, Wenzel observes various differences. Particularly noteworthy is the high ratio of English billboards, which were virtually absent from Tulp's study. However, a direct comparison of the two surveys is problematic because they do not cover the same geographic area. Any conclusions about the diachronic development of Brussels' linguistic landscape therefore remain of a tentative nature.

Concerning the geographic distribution of the two languages Wenzel (1996: 54–60) observed the same tendency as Tulp. While there is a sometimes purely French linguistic landscape in the south, the number of Dutch billboards gradually increases through the northern parts of the survey route. Advertisements in the centre of the city address a more heterogeneous readership, including tourists and foreign business people. This can be gathered from the high rate of English billboards, which in some regions even exceed the number of advertisements in Dutch. At the three train stations the proportion of French and Dutch is more balanced, due to the fact that linguistic equality is legally mandatory in all public facilities in Brussels (Wenzel, 1996: 62–5).

According to Wenzel, the overall dominance of French advertisements in Brussels' linguistic landscape 'reflects the imbalance between the two language groups in the capital'. Especially in the southern parts of the city one gets the impression of being on Walloon territory rather than in an officially bilingual city. The appearance of English in the centre can be interpreted as being motivated by the desire to give the city an 'international' rather than a bilingual outward appearance. Only the situation in the north unambiguously reflects Brussels' bilingual status (Wenzel, 1996: 47, 57, 67).

**Table 3.1** Languages on billboards and shop signs in Brussels

| *Language* | *Frequency* |
|---|---|
| French | 56.5% |
| Dutch | 24.2% |
| English | 9.7% |
| Without text | 7.1% |
| Others | 2.5% |
| **Total** | **100%** |

*Source*: Wenzel (1996: 49)

French dominance of the linguistic landscape is also reflected by the order of the languages on bilingual billboards, where the French part of a text is usually given above the Dutch part. However, the overall ratio of French–Dutch bilingual signs is very low (1.3%), suggesting a 'tendency of strictly separating the two concurring languages from each other'. Though most commercial campaigns are run both in French and Dutch, the two languages usually appear in separate versions (Wenzel, 1996: 67). It is no over-interpretation to consider the strict division of the two languages in their written form as an expression of the continuing conflict between the two language groups in Brussels.

Wenzel also observes correlations between the contents of a commercial sign and the languages used. For instance, English is the language for advertising beverages, cigarettes, and clothes, which Wenzel ascribes to both the internationality of US brands and a tendency to create a 'pseudo-American' image for a product. On the shop signs in the centre of the city English is predominant at shops offering electronic products, while French is favoured in the domain of fashion. Shop signs in Dutch are rare. One example of the inequality between French and Dutch is hairdressers. While French signs announcing an 'institut de beauté' or a 'coiffeur' are a usual sight, Wenzel found not a single 'kapper', which would be the Dutch term (Wenzel, 1996: 50, 58).

One noteworthy type of business is foreign restaurants and shops which put up signs in languages other than French, Dutch, or English. If an additional language apart from these other languages is used, the choice is always made in favour of French. This suggests that Brussels' foreign residents follow the same general patterns of language choice as the city as a whole. With their preference for French they too 'contribute to the un-Dutch street image in the centre of the city' (Wenzel, 1996: 58). In a similar way to Tulp, Wenzel thus emphasises the role of the linguistic landscape in both reflecting and further triggering patterns of language shift, in the case of Brussels in favour of French and to the detriment of Dutch.

## 3.2 Montreal: Controversy Around the *Paysage Linguistique*

Another bilingual environment that shows many similarities to the situation in Brussels is the island of Montreal. Montreal is part of the province of Quebec, Canada. It is dominated by native speakers of French, who at the same time constitute a linguistic minority in English-dominated Canada as a whole. The political and legislative struggle of the Francophone majority for the representation of their language in Quebec began in the 1960s and continues to the present day (Bouchard, 2000; Levine, 1990). It has left its imprints also on the linguistic landscape of Montreal.

A 'legal cornerstone of Québec's language policy' (Dumas, 2002: 156) is the 'Charter of the French Language', also known as Bill 101. Enacted in 1977, it enforces the use of French in legislation and justice, at work, in trade and commerce, and in public administration and education. The Charter also demands that, except for some special cases, all traffic signs, commercial advertisements, and public signs and posters must be in French only. In cases where the use of other languages is permitted, care is taken that French remains the predominant language on a sign. The Charter has been revised several times and become slightly more tolerant towards languages other than French. In 1993, Bill 86 was enacted, which generally permits the presence of other languages on signs both inside and outside shops and other businesses. In such cases, however, French is still obligatory and prescribed to be predominant (CLF, 2000: 4–5; Daoust, 1990: 110–11; for an abridged English version of the Charter see Crawford, 1992: 435–45).

In order to monitor how the regulations of the Charter are being performed in practice, the supervising Council of the French Language (Conseil de la langue française) has administered various types of empirical research. One point of special interest has been the linguistic landscape of Montreal, which was scrutinised in an early study by Monnier (1989). The population of the island by the time of Monnier's research roughly consisted of 60% Francophones (native speakers of French), 20% Anglophones (native speakers of English), and 20% allophones (persons with a native language other than English or French). Concerning the spatial distribution of the linguistic groups, one general trend is a concentration of Anglophone populations in the western part of the island (Monnier, 1989: 10).

Monnier's survey focused on language in the commercial sector. His basic aim was testing in how far language practices in this domain are in line with the legal requirements of the Charter of the French Language. The survey had a two-tiered design, dealing with both spoken and written language. The first part of Monnier's research, which shall be reviewed in more detail, examined language use on shop signs. Monnier (1989: 36) explicitly referred to this aspect as 'paysage linguistique', the linguistic landscape. The survey was conducted between May and June 1988, from Wednesdays to Saturdays between 9.00 a.m. and 9.00 p.m.

Monnier determined 11 survey areas, which he categorised with regard to their inhabitants' linguistic make-up. In these areas, four types of businesses were distinguished: street shops, single shops in shopping centres, department stores, and hotels and restaurants. Counted items were not whole signs but so-called 'information units', that is, coherent phrases such as 'Gâteau aux fruits' or 'Fruit cake', and 'Meilleurs prix' or 'Best low prices'. Contents included were information about the products and services offered, service hours, floors, and security notices. Menus were also included, but counted as one item each rather than being subdivided into smaller information units. The name of a shop or company, brand names, credit card logos, and all information not coming under the direct responsibility of the shopkeeper were excluded from the survey. The exclusion of brand and product names facilitated the linguistic determination of the items since such information units as 'Lampe de poche Eveready' or 'Chaussettes Mcgregor' could be classified unambiguously as French (Monnier, 1989: 14–15, 91).

While the quantitative results of Monnier's survey testify to the overall dominance of French over English in Montreal, his findings differ widely with regard to the type of shop and the geographic distribution of the languages. As to the former point, French was most strongly represented at department stores, where about 90% of all signs were monolingual French. Businesses situated in shopping centres had an average monolingual French outward appearance in 78.3% of the cases, while the same applied to only 59.8% of the street shops (calculated from the figures given in Monnier, 1989: 28). Monolingual French signs were rarest in the domain of hotels and restaurants, with only 39%. Possible reasons for this low ratio are an accommodation to the needs of foreign tourists and the high number of menus containing more than one language (Monnier, 1989: 26–9).

A look at the different survey areas suggests a clear relationship between an area's linguistic population make-up and the languages used on shop signs. French was particularly strong in the east of the island, while the visibility of English signs increased the further one went west. Monolingual French signs were least frequent in the utmost west, where the concentration of Anglophones is highest (Monnier, 1989: 29–36). There is hence a similar relationship between the geographic distribution of the two linguistic groups and the character of the linguistic landscape, as in Brussels. Though this is not a very spectacular insight, it is good to have these correlations empirically testified.

A closer look at the linguistic origin of the owner of a shop revealed some surprising results. According to Monnier (1989: 65, 79) persons with an allophone background more frequently used English on their shop signs than their language of origin. Their proclivity for English was even higher than that of Anglophone shop owners. This is another parallel to the situation in Brussels, where shopkeepers of foreign origin have shown a clear preference for French over Dutch.

The second part of Monnier's study dealt with the language spoken inside a shop. Points in question were the language of the employee when addressing a customer on entering the shop and the general availability of French-speaking staff. Combining the two parts of the survey, Monnier (1989: 54) observed a relationship between the language written outside a shop and the language spoken inside. It is as though 'the language used by the employees for welcoming customers is already partially inscribed into the signs of the shop windows.' The signs in the streets thus do more than just transport a linguistic content. At the same time they contain a message about the owner of the sign.

The Council of the French Language has continued conducting research into Montreal's linguistic landscape. It commissioned further surveys in 1995, 1996, 1997, and 1999. In order to monitor the diachronic development of Montreal's linguistic landscape, a unified methodology was developed to allow for a direct comparison of the results from different years. This methodology had to be slightly revised before being applied in exactly the same way in the surveys from 1997 and 1999. The results of these two surveys are summarised in a publication edited by the Council of the French Language (CLF, 2000), which also discusses various methodological details about the collection of the data.

A first important point is the determination of the survey areas. In order to get a geographically representative sample, areas were selected using arbitrarily chosen postal codes and addresses. Each survey area was defined as one side of a street on which one of the determined addresses was positioned. It was spatially confined by intersections on each side. Within the survey areas the signs of each second business were counted. It was further determined that, if an area contained fewer than five businesses, every business was to be counted. If there were more than 25 businesses in the area, only every fourth business was counted. The eventual number of businesses recorded amounted to over 3100.

Another problem to be solved was the determination of countable items. All signs had to belong to shops or other businesses in the streets and be visible from outside. Similar to Monnier, though without direct reference to his study, the Council decided not to count whole signs but 'messages', defined as 'information unit[s] consisting of one or several words'. The entity chosen was determined on the basis not of physical but semantic categories. It could coincide with the physical boundaries of a sign but also could be smaller or larger. The Council gives examples to demonstrate their suggested way of counting (CLF, 2000: 7–8). Thus, the following sign contains three countable messages:

```
FREINS
SOUDURE ÉLECTRIQUE
TRANSMISSION STANDARD
```

The next example consists of three signs, but there is only one message to be counted, given twice in French and once in English:

```
SOLDE      SOLDE      SALES
```

To simplify the counting of the items the term 'list' was introduced, referring to those signs structured in list format. Each list was counted as only one message. An example is given below:

```
ESCOMPTES

•  Cosmétiques
•  Parfums
•  Cartes de souhaits
```

A third methodological problem concerns the determination of the languages. It was decided that proper names of brands, companies, etc., should be categorised as 'indeterminable'. Though the introduction of this category simplifies the overall procedure of data collection, it involves some problems. As the Council acknowledges, most of the messages categorised as 'indeterminable' were likely to contain English and would be perceived so by most passers-by. However, they do not appear as English messages in the statistics, which may give a less anglicised picture of the situation than there actually is (CLF, 2000: 32).

The results of the two surveys will be only briefly summarised here. An important motivation for the Council's research into the linguistic landscape has been assessing the degree of legal conformity to the requirement that French be the language predominant on all commercial signs. In this respect, all businesses with even only one sign not containing French (e.g. 'OPEN' on an entrance door) were considered to fail to comply with current legislation. A direct comparison of the two surveys from 1997 and 1999 revealed a statistically significant increase of businesses whose signs did not agree with the regulations made by the Charter of the French Language. While 79.5% of all businesses followed the rules in 1997, the rate was down to 75.8% in 1999 (CLF, 2000: 32).

The same tendency was found with regard to the general presence of English on shop signs, including those cases where its use did not constitute a violation of the law. The comparison of the two surveys showed a decrease in businesses that had only French messages on their signs from 52% to 47%, combined with an increase in businesses making use of both French and English messages from 37% to 43%. Moreover, a growing number of businesses with messages characterised as 'indeterminable' suggests an increase of messages containing English, too (CLF, 2000: 34–7).

The Council finally analysed the total of the recorded messages, regardless of their distribution at the respective businesses. The increase of English to the detriment of French is observable here, too. Table 3.2 gives a comparison of the 24,916 messages of 1997 and the 25,741 messages of 1999. It shows statistically significant shifts concerning the share of

**Table 3.2** 'Messages' on shop signs in Montreal

| Languages | 1997 | 1999 |
|---|---|---|
| French only | 73.3% | 69.0% |
| Undetermined | 13.1% | 14.4% |
| French and English equal | 5.9% | 7.1% |
| English only | 4.5% | 5.8% |
| More French than English | 1.3% | 1.9% |
| Others | 1.9% | 1.8% |
| Total | 100% | 100% |

*Source*: CLF (2000: 51)

French-only messages, messages with balanced presence of French and English, English-only messages, indeterminable messages, and messages without French (CLF, 2000: 49–53). These, as all other observations concerning the diachronic development of Montreal's linguistic land-scape, are feasible only because of the Council's refined methodology of data collection.

In general, the extensive legal measures concerning the graphic representation of the French language in Montreal testify to the high relevance ascribed to the role of written language in public space. As Levine points out in his book *The Reconquest of Montreal*:

> The sign issue is symbolically explosive. Many Montreal Franco-phones see anything short of unilingual French signs as the contin-uing legacy of the 'Conquest', while Anglophones view bilingual signs as a symbol that Montreal is a 'social contract' between two linguistic communities. In short, the debate over Montreal's 'French face' revolves around antithetical visions of the city: Montreal as a fundamentally French city versus Montreal as a dualistic city. (1990: 137)

Different practices of language use on signs represent different views on the linguistic regime of a place. Monnier (1989: 83–4) complains in his concluding remarks that the results of his study show that the situation in Montreal is not as monolingual French as, in view of the overall dominance of the Francophones, it should be expected to be. Back in Brussels, on the other hand, Tulp demands that the quantitative representation of French and Dutch be evenly balanced irrespective of the different demographic strengths of the two linguistic groups. A juxta-position of the two points of view strikingly reveals how similar situations of linguistic conflict can be interpreted in completely opposite ways depending on which side you're on – majority or minority.

### 3.3 Jerusalem: Signs of Power, Signs of Solidarity

Jerusalem faces much graver problems than linguistic struggle between two population groups. The fact that the city is of high spiritual importance to the world's three major monotheistic religions has entailed numerous ethnic, religious, and geopolitical conflicts throughout history. They continue to the present day. Shortly after the foundation of the State of Israel in May 1948, parts of the city were occupied by then Transjordanian troops and the city became divided into Israeli (West Jerusalem) and Jordanian (East Jerusalem) sectors. During the Six-Day War in 1967 the eastern parts were taken by Israeli troops and the city as a whole was proclaimed the capital of the State of Israel. Nevertheless, the city's status has remained a point of international contention.

Present-day Jerusalem has traits of a bilingual city. Its western parts are dominated by Hebrew-speaking groups, whereas the eastern parts, including the Old City, are mainly inhabited by Arab populations. Both Hebrew and Arabic have official status in Israel. English is a third language of major importance. It was the official language from when the British accepted a mandate from the League of Nations to administer Palestine until the new state's independence in 1948. To the present day, English is used for many government functions. It is also a compulsory subject in public schools. Due to continuing migration movements to Israel a great variety of other languages are in frequent use. The degree of both individual and societal multilingualism is high (Spolsky, 1997; Spolsky & Shohamy, 1999).

An early survey into the linguistic landscape of Jerusalem was carried out in 1973 in a street called Keren Kayemet Street (Rosenbaum *et al.*, 1977). It was part of a larger study whose underlying research interest was to explore to what extent English in Jerusalem was available and directly encountered in public. Keren Kayemet Street is situated in the western, Jewish-dominated part of the city. By the time of Rosenbaum *et al.*'s research it was for more than half of its length a narrow and busy street. With about 30 shops, 3 restaurants, 10 private offices, and 9 government offices, this section of the street was determined as the research area. The authors acknowledged that the selected area was not representative of Jerusalem as a whole. Due to its geographic position, the proportion of passers-by who could be assumed to have some proficiency in English was likely to be higher than in most other parts of the city. Keren Kayemet Street thus yields an upper limit to the estimated degree to which English is used in the streets of Jerusalem.

The authors worked with a small corpus of 50 signs, each of which contained the name of an establishment (shop, office, etc.) and the type of goods or services offered. The signs were linguistically classified according to the prominence of the Roman alphabet. Three types were distinguished: signs with Roman and Hebrew script in equal proportion; signs with some Roman script but with Hebrew script clearly dominating; and signs with no Roman script at all. Signs with more Roman than Hebrew script or with other scripts were not found. Rosenbaum *et al.* interpreted use of the Roman script as being tantamount to the use of English. The authors justified this procedure by the fact that virtually all words written in Roman script, except for proper names, were English words. The results of their analysis are given in Table 3.3.

The three types of signs were quantitatively almost equally distributed, but the authors observed some noteworthy correlations between the appearance of the Roman alphabet and the type of establishment using the sign. While the signs of the grocery stores and kiosks were exclusively in Hebrew, Hebrew-only signs were used by less than one-third of the other shops. A possible interpretation of this outcome is that the higher the per-unit cost of the merchandise or service offered the more likely will be the use of English. The underlying motivation by the producer of the sign is exploiting the 'snob appeal' of the English language (Rosenbaum *et al.*, 1977: 187).

A second tendency is that the Roman script was more prominent on signs of private offices, all of which contained at least some alphabet elements, than on those of public offices, where one-third of all signs were in Hebrew only. Though the total number of cases on which this observation is based is rather small, this finding suggests a considerable gap

> between the official language policy, which was set at the independence of the State and which stresses the dominance of the national language, and the much higher tolerance towards foreign languages in general and English in particular that is expected by the general public today. (Rosenbaum *et al.*, 1977: 189)

**Table 3.3** Signs in West Jerusalem

| Type of business | Roman equal to Hebrew script | Less Roman than Hebrew script | No Roman script |
|---|---|---|---|
| Grocery stores and kiosks | – | – | 6 |
| Shops offering services | 1 | 2 | 2 |
| Other shops | 8 | 4 | 5 |
| Restaurants | 1 | 1 | 1 |
| Public offices | 1 | 5 | 3 |
| Private offices | 6 | 4 | – |
| **Total** | **17** | **16** | **17** |

*Source*: Rosenbaum *et al.* (1977: 188)

The other parts of Rosenbaum *et al.*'s study focused on the spoken use of English in public space. Data were collected about conversations in the street and, in a similar way to Monnier (1989) in Montreal, language use of the shopkeepers. Combining the different parts of the survey, an overall outcome of Rosenbaum *et al.*'s research was that English could be seen as well as heard on Keren Kayemet Street, but it was relatively more seen than heard.

Linguistic landscape research in the eastern parts of Jerusalem was conducted by Spolsky and Cooper (1991), who collected data about language use on the signs in the Old City. Working with a sample of 339 items, Spolsky and Cooper were particularly interested in the motivations that account for language usage patterns on signs in this part of Jerusalem. In other words: 'What language or languages, and in what order, appear on the signs, and how can this choice be explained?' (1991: 76).

A first methodological problem was how to determine the languages of the signs. Unlike Rosenbaum *et al.* (1977), the authors did not classify the signs on the basis of the script(s) they contained. A helpful distinction in this respect, particularly with regard to toponymic signs, is that between transliteration and translation. Transliteration refers to the conversion of the graphemes of one writing system into those of another, for instance from Hebrew script into Roman script. Translation is the result of transferring a text from a source language into a target language, for instance Hebrew into English. In the streets of Jerusalem Spolsky and Cooper found a mixture of both strategies. In 'BAB EL-JADID RD.' or 'OMAR IBN EL-KHATTAB SQ.', for instance, a Roman transliteration of the Arabic terms is combined with an English abbreviation for the place to be designated. Both complete transliterations, as in 'QABAT KHAN EL-AQBAT' for 'Street of the Copts', and complete translations, as in 'WESTERN WALL RD.', occasionally occurred, too (Spolsky & Cooper, 1991: 74–5).

The 339 signs of Spolsky and Cooper's sample contained 12 languages: Hebrew, Arabic, English, Armenian, French, German, Aramaic, Greek, Italian, Latin, Coptic, and Swedish. The three languages most frequently used were Hebrew, English, and Arabic. While this reflects major characteristics of the linguistic make-up of the city, Spolsky and Cooper also emphasise that it 'omits a significant number of thirty or so languages that people in the Old City claim to speak' (1991: 81). In order to find out why some languages but not others appear on the signs of the city, Spolsky and Cooper introduce a preference model based on three components: (1) a 'sign-writer's skill' condition, (2) a 'presumed reader' condition, and (3) a 'symbolic value' condition (Spolsky & Cooper, 1991: 81–5).

The 'sign-writer's skill' condition refers to the necessity of the one who produces a sign to know the language chosen. It simply says: 'Write signs in a language you know.' This may appear self-evident were it not for a number of grammatical and orthographic errors in Spolsky and Cooper's sample, which witness that knowledge of a language is a gradual phenomenon. The 'presumed reader' condition demands that the language to be used be intelligible to those the message is intended to address. Especially if a sign is put up for commercial reasons, the sign writer may prefer a language understood by potential customers even in cases where the sign writer's skill condition is only partially met.

While the first two conditions are practically motivated, the 'symbolic value' condition has a political or socio-psychological background. The underlying aim is a desire to assert power ('By controlling the languages of the sign, I declare power over the space designated') or to claim solidarity or identity ('My statement of socio-cultural membership is in the language I have chosen'). The 'symbolic value' condition says: 'Prefer to write signs in your own language or in a language with which you wish to be identified'. Rather than a content to be transferred by means of a sign, it is choice of the language itself that becomes the message. A negative application of condition (3) is observable when the language of a certain group of assumed readers is intentionally not used on a sign. One example is former trilingual Hebrew–Arabic–English signs at police stations that were replaced by bilingual signs in English and Hebrew. As Spolsky and Cooper comment on the disuse of Arabic and its implications:

> The use of these bilingual police signs, on which one of the languages is not an official language, is doubly insulting: there is room for two languages, but there is no room for Arabic . . . To Arab residents of the Old City the bilingual police signs give a clear message: the Old City, in which you are a majority, is not under your control; this police station, staffed primarily by Arab policemen, is not your station; this state is not your state. (1991: 116–17, emphasis original)

Applying the three conditions to a study sample of 91 signs, Spolsky and Cooper observed that in almost 60% of the cases condition (1) applied. This means that, for the majority of the signs, the first or only language chosen can be assumed to be that of the sign writer. The authors further mention that 'in most cases' the first or only language chosen is at the same time that of the assumed sign reader, so that both conditions (1) and (2) are followed. Interesting are those cases of the sample where the symbolic value condition applies but not the assumed reader condition. Signs of this sort, which were mainly found attached to buildings owned by foreign institutions, convey the message that 'proclaiming ownership is more important than being understood' (Spolsky & Cooper, 1991: 81–5).

Spolsky and Cooper (1991: 5–8) also deal with diachronic issues of the Old City's linguistic landscape. In the course of their survey they came across three different versions of a tiled street sign, each of them representing a different stage in Jerusalem's recent history. The oldest type of sign dated from the period of the British Mandate (1922–48), which could be inferred from the order of the languages. The English, Arabic, and Hebrew inscriptions were arranged from top to bottom in this order. The two other signs both gave Hebrew on top, Arabic in the middle line, and English at the bottom. A closer inspection, however, revealed some subtle differences between the two. Thus, whereas the frieze border around the tiles in one case enclosed the whole sign, in the other case there were actually two friezes, one around the Hebrew part and one around the Arabic–English part. Spolsky and Cooper assumed that the latter sign originally used to be a bilingual Arabic–English sign that was put up when the eastern parts of the city were under Jordanian rule (1948–67). The Hebrew version in a separate frieze on top must have been added after Israel gained power over the Old City in 1967. All signs produced after that time use only one frieze for all three languages, just like the third type of sign Spolsky and Cooper found.

Another difference between the two Hebrew–Arabic–English street signs was that the English version contained different transliterations. In the case of the sign from the Jordanian period it was modelled after the Arabic toponym ('EL-MALAK RD.'), while the sign produced after 1967 gave a transliteration of the Hebrew term ('HA-MALAKH RD.'). Changes in the Old City's linguistic landscape thus do not only refer to the order of languages on signs, but to transliteration practices as well. Determining what is to be considered the original language of a sign from which accompanying other versions are derived is a subtle but unmistakable way of indicating who is in charge of a given territory.

Language use on signs in the streets of Jerusalem has continued to attract sociolinguistic attention. Recently, a third study has been conducted by Ben-Rafael *et al*. (2004, 2006). Their empirical research in East and West Jerusalem is part of a larger project into the linguistic landscape of Israel. Its aim is to examine how language use on signs reflects Jewish–Arab multilingualism in Israel and what underlying forces are involved in shaping the linguistic landscape. Ben-Rafael *et al*. work with a sample of more than 1000 signs, which were recorded by digital camera at eight locations throughout Israel. These include neighbourhoods in East and West Jerusalem, Tel Aviv, Nazareth, and some smaller cities and towns. The places chosen can be classified as inhabited predominantly either by Jews or by Israeli Palestinians. The survey area in East Jerusalem is an exception in that the population to large parts consists of Arabs who have not accepted to become Israeli citizens but chose to retain Jordanian nationality instead.

A quantitative analysis of the languages contained on the signs of the sample shows that Hebrew is the language most frequently found both in areas dominated by Jews and in areas dominated by Israeli Palestinians. A major difference between the two types of environments is the use of Arabic, which is contained on the majority of signs in Israeli Palestinian areas but is found only sporadically in Jewish areas. This situation is reversed in East Jerusalem, where Hebrew is weakly represented and appears only in combination with Arabic or on trilingual Hebrew–Arabic–English signs. Arabic, on the other hand, is omnipresent, appearing either in combination or alone on all signs recorded. The linguistic landscape of East Jerusalem reflects its exceptional socio-political status (Ben-Rafael *et al.*, 2004: 22–5; 2006: 16–19). The data are given in Table 3.4.

Another important variable is the official or non-official background of a sign. Ben-Rafael *et al.* (2004: 17; 2006: 14) make a basic distinction between 'top-down' and 'bottom-up' flows of linguistic landscape components. The former notion refers to signs issued by the state or by central bureaucracies, while 'bottom-up' signs are signs set up by autonomous actors such as shop owners, companies, or other private enterprises.

The two types of signs reveal different characteristics of language use with regard to the respective research areas. While there is no recognisable difference between bottom-up and top-down flows in the Jewish-dominated locations, the survey areas mainly inhabited by Israeli Palestinians show a rather unexpected trend. The largest group of bottom-up signs in these locations are Hebrew-only signs rather than signs containing Arabic. In East Jerusalem, by contrast, Hebrew occurs almost exclusively on officially issued top-down signs. This suggests that Hebrew

**Table 3.4** Signs at three types of Israeli locations

|  | Localities | | |
|---|---|---|---|
|  | *Jews* (*n* = 680) | *Israeli Palestinians* (*n* = 241) | *East Jerusalem* (*n* = 86) |
| Hebrew only | 49.6% | 24.1% | – |
| Arabic only | 0.1% | 5.0% | 20.9% |
| Hebrew/English | 44.6% | 6.2% | – |
| Hebrew/Arabic | 0.9% | 39.4% | 5.8% |
| Arabic/English | – | 1.2% | 55.8% |
| Hebrew/Arabic/English | 4.9% | 24.1% | 17.4% |
| **Total** | **100%** | **100%** | **100%** |

*Source*: Ben-Rafael *et al.* (2004: 22; 2006: 17)

in East Jerusalem is imposed by the state, whereas at the other locations dominated by Arabic-speaking populations it is integrated into the linguistic landscape by the citizens themselves (Ben-Rafael *et al.*, 2004: 25–7; 2006: 19–21).

One basic conclusion of Ben-Rafael *et al.*'s study is that the linguistic landscape in Israel reflects a linguistic 'asymmetry in Arab–Jewish relations, where Jews are largely monolingual whereas Arabs are bilingual in Arabic and Hebrew' (2004: 32). This asymmetry is implied particularly by the weak representation of signs containing Arabic in Jewish localities, in contradistinction to the salience of signs in Hebrew, even on bottom-up signs, in survey areas dominated by Palestinian Israelis. The situation in East Jerusalem with its high visibility of Arabic and a virtual absence of Hebrew from bottom-up signs is a noteworthy exception, suggesting differing language attitudes within the group of Palestinians in Israel. As Ben-Rafael *et al.* summarise:

> In brief, L[inguistic] L[andscape] analysis reveals two contrastive models of two groups belonging to the same minority within the same majority group. These two groups see themselves as members of the same Palestinian people and share the same language and culture; moreover, they do have close contacts with each other, though, and due to their different positioning in the society, they develop very different relations with the same Jewish majority. (2006: 25–6)

The three approaches discussed in this section show that Jerusalem has been one of the key locations for research into the linguistic landscape. As will be seen in subsequent sections, many of the points explored by Rosenbaum *et al.* in the 1970s, Spolsky and Cooper in the 1980s, and recently Ben-Rafael *et al.* have been taken up in similar ways by other researchers around the globe. The example discussed in the next section is one such case.

## 3.4 Ljouwert and Donostia: Two Other Linguistic Landscapes of Europe

The two cities Ljouwert and Donostia have been research sites of a recent linguistic landscape study by Cenoz and Gorter (2006). It is a comparative approach to the visibility of two regional European minority languages in public space. Ljouwert is the capital of the Dutch province Friesland, where Frisian is formally recognised as second official language. It is a city of approximately 90,000 inhabitants, referred to in Dutch as Leeuwarden. Donostia is situated in the Basque Country in the north of Spain and has a population of around 180,000 people. Its Spanish name is San Sebastián. Basque and Spanish have been official languages in the Basque Autonomous Community since 1979 (Cenoz & Gorter, 2006: 68–70).

In the centre of interest of Cenoz and Gorter's research is how the two minority languages Frisian and Basque in the linguistic landscape of the two locations concur with the two national languages Dutch and Spanish on one hand, and with English as the most important international language on the other. Their methodology follows Rosenbaum *et al.*'s (1977) approach, which has been discussed in section 3.3. In each of the two locations one shopping street of approximately 600 metres in length was chosen, in which the complete inventory of signs was recorded by digital camera. A total of 975 photos were taken and subsequently summarised into 207 'units of analysis'. Rather than each single sign, the whole sign inventory of an establishment was considered relevant, because 'each text belongs to a larger whole instead of being clearly separate'. This methodology resembles the approach by the Council of the French Language in Montreal (see 3.2), though no direct reference is made. Single items that could not be classified to be part of a specific establishment were categorised as 'others' (Cenoz & Gorter, 2006: 71).

Partially based on the framework by Ben-Rafael *et al.* (2006; see 3.3), Cenoz and Gorter analyse their two samples with regard to the following questions: whether a unit of analysis contains one language or more; what languages are contained; which language is displayed in prominent position ('first language') or in larger size ('size of text'); what 'type of font' is used; what 'amount of information' is given in each language; and whether or not the languages used constitute translations of each other ('translation in bi/multilingual signs').

Table 3.5 gives the basic results concerning the languages contained and their combinations in the two survey areas. Over 60% of the establishments in Ljouwert use only one language for public display, which in most cases is Dutch. The second-strongest pattern is a combination of Dutch and English, which was identified in 31% of the cases. Frisian is represented very weakly only. Only 3% of the cases are monolingual Frisian, while another 2% are combinations of Frisian and Dutch. The analysed units in Donostia give a more balanced picture. Equivalent to Ljouwert, the most frequent pattern is Spanish only (36%). However, it is followed by a combination of Basque and Spanish (22%), Basque only (12%), and units of Basque, Spanish, and English signs (10%).

While there is thus little variation with regard to the dominance of the two national languages, Dutch and Spanish, the degree of visibility of the two regional languages in the linguistic landscapes of the two places is different. Whereas Basque is clearly present, Frisian is hardly visible at all. The fact that, in exchange, English is more prominent in Ljouwert than in Donostia suggests reversed patterns of language preference with regard to regional language and English in the two places (Cenoz & Gorter, 2006: 72–4).

**Table 3.5** Signs in two shopping streets in Ljouwert (Netherlands) and
Donostia (Spain)

| *Languages/combinations* | *Ljouwert* | *Donostia* |
|---|---|---|
| Frisian; | 3% | – |
| Basque | – | 12% |
| Dutch; | 53% | – |
| Spanish | – | 36% |
| Frisian + Dutch; | 2% | – |
| Basque + Spanish | – | 22% |
| Dutch + English; | 31% | – |
| Spanish + English | – | 6% |
| English | 6% | 4% |
| Basque + Spanish + English | – | 10% |
| Others | 5% | 10% |
| **Total** | **100%** | **100%** |

*Source*: Cenoz and Gorter (2006: 73)


The same tendency was observed in most of the other analytical categories applied by Cenoz and Gorter. For instance, while Frisian is hardly
ever the prominent language in a unit of analysis in Ljouwert, Basque
holds this position in 28% of the cases in Donostia. With respect to
English, prominent on 20% of the Ljouwert items but on only 5% in the
Donosita sample, the situation is reversed. The size of the languages,
categorised into 'all the same', 'minority bigger', 'majority bigger',
'majority and minority bigger', and 'majority and foreign bigger', show
a similar trend (Cenoz & Gorter, 2006: 74–6).

Apart from the languages contained and their visual arrangement,
Cenoz and Gorter also take a closer look at the availability of translation in those units of their sample containing more than one language.
Most of the relevant entities in Ljouwert do not contain translations of
each other but give disparate contents. In Donostia, by contrast, mutual
translation, either word for word or in part, can be found on the overall
majority of the items. This contrast is interpreted as indicative of a variety
of differences between the two locations, particular with regard to official language policies and the linguistic profiles of the population. As
Cenoz and Gorter summarise:

> There is no official language policy of dual language use in Friesland.
> The official policy has been for many years an 'either or' system for
> language choice. Official government documents are published either

in Dutch, or in Frisian. Using both Frisian and Dutch side by side in literal translation was seen as superfluous, because all inhabitants of Friesland were supposed to be able to read both languages . . .

The linguistic distance between Spanish and Basque is much larger [than between Dutch and Frisian] and the official policy has been from the beginning to make all kinds of documents available in both languages. Even though the whole population can read Spanish, the translation is not considered superfluous. The official policy is reflected in the linguistic landscape not only in the case of official top-down signs but also in many cases when bottom-up signs are considered. (2006: 77)

Availability and non-availability of translation is an important analytical category in linguistic landscape research, which so far has received only minor attention. The potential of this type of analysis will be discussed in more detail in section 3.6.

In sum, Cenoz and Gorter's comparative approach reveals some clear differences with regard to language preference patterns in the trilingual context of a regional language, a national language, and an international language in two of Western Europe's 'other' linguistic landscapes. The next section discusses one more comparative approach to language on signs.

## 3.5 Paris and Dakar: The Walls Speak

Paris and Dakar have in common that they have been destinations of constant migration movements due to which they have become linguistically highly diversified places. They differ in that the multilingual profile of the French capital is a result of international migration, while linguistic diversity in Dakar is predominantly brought about by population influxes from other parts of Senegal. The two cities and their linguistic landscapes have been examined and compared in an earlier study by Calvet (1990, 1994).

One characteristic of the linguistic landscape of Paris is that, irrespective of their demographic strength, some linguistic groups make their presence felt visually more than others. Thus, there are hardly any signs in Spanish or Portuguese, even in areas where larger Spanish- and Portuguese-speaking populations are known to reside. Signs containing Asian scripts or Arabic writing, on the other hand, have become a distinctive part of the city's linguistic landscape. They are particularly prominent in the Belleville quarter, where major populations of the Asian and North African community live (Calvet, 1990: 76).

A noteworthy point made by Calvet refers to the underlying intentions for language use on signs. One example is Chinese characters, for which he observes two essentially different motivations. Writings at the front of a typical Parisian Chinese restaurant are simply intended to indicate to all passers-by that Chinese food is served here. Rather than the content of the message – often merely the name of the restaurant, it is the visibility of the Chinese characters itself that is of importance. Even though the majority of Parisian passers-by will not be able to read Chinese, they will recognise the 'air chinois' about the business. Writing on signs of a Chinese restaurant in the Belleville area, by contrast, is directly addressed to people who are expected to know the language. Chinese information given on these signs is not confined to a Chinese version of the restaurant's name, but also contains details about the menu, the origin of the owner, etc. Calvet (1990: 76) holds that language on this latter type of sign is intended to convey a linguistic content, whereas in the former case the content of the message is of minor importance and language is mainly used as an index of the sign writer.

Calvet's research about the linguistic landscape of Dakar starts with a brief introduction to the linguistic make-up of the city. Both on the individual and on the societal level the situation in the Senegalese capital is highly multilingual. The majority of the population speak Wolof, which coexists with the official language French, Arabic as the language of religion, and several minority languages exclusively used within the family. These minority languages are predominantly spoken by migrants recently moved to the city, whose proficiency in Wolof and French is lower than that of people born in Dakar. Wolof has acquired characteristics of a 'language of integration', while French is considered the 'language of power' (Calvet, 1994: 208). This unequal relationship is reflected in Dakar's linguistic landscape.

An important distinction Calvet makes (also 1993: 112–13) is that between 'in vitro' and 'in vivo' aspects of the linguistic landscape. In a similar way as Ben-Rafael *et al.*'s (2004, 2006; see 3.3) classification of 'top-down' and 'bottom-up' signs, the two terms distinguish between what is written in vitro by the state (toponymic signs, traffic signs, etc.) and what is written in vivo by the citizens (shop signs, graffiti, advertisements, etc.). The two types of signs constitute 'two different ways of *marking the territory*, two inscriptions into the urban space' (Calvet, 1990: 75, emphasis original).

The in vivo parts of Dakar's linguistic landscape reflect the basic features of the city's linguistic conditions. Calvet finds three languages, French, Arabic, and Wolof, and two scripts, Roman and Arabic, on the walls of the city. The visible coexistence of the three languages and their scripts can be explained with the different functions assigned to each of them. French is the official language, Wolof serves as lingua franca, and Arabic is the language of religion. The in vitro parts of Dakar's linguistic landscape, however, give a different picture of the city's linguistic make-up. Official signs contain no other languages apart from the official language, French. This reveals a similar gap between official language policies and everyday linguistic practices as observed by Rosenbaum *et al.* (1977; see 3.3) on Keren Kayemet Street in Jerusalem.

One characteristic feature of the linguistic landscape of Dakar is script contact. In this respect, Calvet observes various instances of instability with regard to the languages involved and their graphic representation. Arabic texts appear not necessarily in Arabic letters but occasionally in the Roman alphabet, too. Likewise, Wolof is found in either Roman or Arabic script. According to Calvet, this state of 'insecurity' between language and script is indicative of a situation between orality and literacy in Dakar. Similar observations in Paris could not be made. The linguistic landscape thus suggests differences between the multi-lingualisms of the two cities. As Calvet summarises:

> Thus, in Paris as in Dakar, the walls of the city speak to those who can see and decipher them. But in these two situations we do not at all have the same types of relationships between form and content, between *graphic form* – that is, choice of this or that writing system (Chinese characters; Roman, Arabic, Vietnamese, etc., alphabet) – and *linguistic content* – that is, use of this or that language. In Paris, the relationships are unambiguous, the choice of the language deter-mining that of the script: French is written in the Roman alphabet, Arabic in the Arabic alphabet ... and Chinese in Chinese charac-ters. In Dakar, the relationships between language and script are more fluctuant and give proof, as we have said, of a situation of transition from orality to literacy of a society in which the relation-ships to the script are not really fixed. (1994: 267–8, emphasis original)

Calvet's comparison of the linguistic landscapes of Paris and Dakar shows how language use on signs can be read as reflecting similarities and differences of two multilingual cities in officially monolingual states in Europe and Africa.

## 3.6 Lira Town: Multilingual Signs and How to Read Them

Another example of linguistic landscape research on the African conti-nent is Reh's (2004) study of Lira Town, a municipality of around 27,000 inhabitants in the north of Uganda. The majority of the population in Lira Town speak varieties of Lango, summarised in Uganda under the term Lwo. Uganda has about 40 indigenous languages, which coexist with English as the country's only official language. Lwo is used at lower primary school level, but all subsequent formal education is in English (Reh, 2004: 3).

For a closer analysis of Lira's linguistic landscape Reh (2004: 3–15) introduces a methodological framework based on three parameters: (1) the spatial mobility of the object inscribed, (2) the visibility of the multilingual nature of a sign, and (3) the functional arrangement of multilingual information. Concerning spatial mobility, the carrier of a text can be either stationary or mobile. Stationary carriers include the fronts of buildings, trees, signboards, poles, and all other sorts of backgrounds for physically fixed written announcements. Characteristic types of mobile carriers are newspapers and books, inscribed commodities exposed in front of shops, vehicles like buses and cars, T-shirts, etc.

The two types of carriers entail different reading conditions. Stationary carriers presuppose a mobile reader, whom otherwise the message would not reach. If the text on a stationary carrier contains information limited in its relevance to the place where it has been set up (e.g. regulatory signs), it will remain without consequence if reader and message do not come together. If, however, the information given is not directly related to its environment, like for instance advertisements, a text on an immobile carrier 'attains its communicative goals only if the potential readership is mobile or if the text is repeated in a large number of locations' (Reh, 2004: 4). The underlying problem is in how far the meaning of a sign rests on the environment where it has been set up, a point already discussed in the previous chapter.

The second parameter introduced by Reh (2004: 5–7) is based on the question of whether or not the multilingual nature of a text is visible. If different versions of a text are given on separate carriers, a message is available in more than one language but its multilingual nature is not visible to the reader. Reh refers to this option as 'covert multilingualism'. Multilingualism becomes visible when different versions of a text appear on one carrier. For a closer analysis of this latter type of multilingual writing, Reh introduces a third parameter. She distinguishes four alternatives: duplicating, fragmentary, overlapping, and complementary multilingual writing. Duplicating multilingual writing means that a text appears on a sign in exactly the same wording in two or more languages. Fragmentary multilingual writing applies when the full content of a message is given in one language only, but selected parts have been translated into at least one other language. If two or more languages on a sign give partially the same information but additionally convey different contents each, the multilingualism is overlapping. Finally, it is complementary if the languages used contain different but complementary information so that, for a full understanding of the message, proficiency in more than one language is required.

Reh's third parameter can be used to make hypotheses about individual and societal language proficiencies. In the case of complementary multilingual writing, for instance, a competent multilingual group of readers is presupposed, while the appearance of duplicating multilingual writing would suggest societal multilingualism but individual monolingualism (Reh, 2004: 8–15).

Applying the theoretical framework to the situation in Lira Town, Reh identifies some general trends with regard to the languages used, their communicative functions, and their appearance in different social domains. The city is dominated by English texts, ubiquitous on all signs of official buildings, shop signs, advertisements, and many other types of signs. Signs containing texts in Lwo are much rarer in Lira Town. Their letter size is smaller than that of English texts and they appear exclusively in non-governmental contexts. Lwo is rarely used monolingually but normally comes in combination with English. In most of these cases the two languages are organised in a complementary or overlapping fashion. According to Reh's methodological framework, this indicates individual bilingualism by larger sections of Lira's literate population. The fact that the Lwo part of the signs tends to be more complex in grammatical structure suggests that individual language proficiency is higher in Lwo than in English. This assumption is further corroborated by the general trend to restrict 'dialogue-stimulating' sentence types such as requests and questions, as well as all forms of allusions, irony, and word play, to the Lwo part of the sign. Languages other than Lwo or English are hardly visible in Lira Town at all (Reh, 2004: 17–28).

Reh (2004: 28–38) further observes correlations between language use and various domains, that is, types of shops, businesses, establishments, etc. Both government-related institutions and non-governmental organisations exclusively use monolingual English signs. Other domains where English texts are predominant are the health sector, stationery and book shops, photocopying and computer services, and non-local advertising. Banks used to have only monolingual English signs, too, but since 2002 some information in Lwo has come into use. One such example discussed by Reh is a poster about money transfer procedures. The text on the poster also reveals specific problems involved in written language contact. While some terms of English origin in the Lwo text are given in their original spelling ('account', 'bank', 'draft', etc.), other English loans such as 'cukul' for 'school', or 'opici' for 'office' have been rendered into Lwo orthography.

One domain where Lwo is represented more strongly than English is the agricultural sector. It uses signs with Lwo-dominated English–Lwo texts and even provides for some monolingual Lwo signs. Other domains frequently making use of Lwo are drug stores and water kiosks, shops offering everyday commodities, and warning notices. This distribution suggests certain regularities underlying the use of Lwo and English. Reh observes a social dichotomy between official and local language:

The pervasive link between the use of written Lwo and the agricultural sector and simple everyday needs on the one hand, and monolingualism in English with administration, education, modern communicative technology, and commodities for the wealthier segment of customers reinforces a dichotomy between Lwo and English, in which the use of Lwo is attributed to and becomes associated with daily routine while English is attributed to and becomes associated with the modern economic sector and social and economic advancement. Such a dichotomy easily results in a negative view of the local language if it is not used in modern administration, education, and economy, and in the interpretation that the language is generally not suitable for such purposes. (2004: 39)

At the same time, however, Reh also sees first instances counteracting the dichotomous relationship between the two languages. One example is posters of elections and political campaigns, which have come to be produced in a bilingual format. In addition, there is a recent tendency for national and international companies to promote their products in local languages. An example already mentioned is Lwo signs at banks; another example discussed is Coca Cola advertisement posters almost exclusively using Lwo. Democracy and rise of a market economy are the underlying global forces Reh (2004: 37–8) identifies to be cautiously breaking up the functional dichotomy between English and Lwo. In domains where all layers of the literate population are considered relevant potential readers – as voters or as consumers – a dichotomous language use is unlikely to yield positive results. Though difficult to quantify without a fixed sample of signs, Reh's study hence includes a hypothesis about how to read the diachronic development of Lira Town's linguistic landscape.

## 3.7 Hong Kong, Beijing, Vienna, Paris, Washington: Semiotic Aggregates

A contribution to the study of the linguistic landscape particularly relevant from a theoretical point of view has recently been made by Scollon and Scollon (2003), who have explored language use on signs at various places around the world. Scollon and Scollon consider any given piece of cityscape to be a 'semiotic aggregate' formed of a multiplicity of discourses. Language on signs makes up a large part of these discourses, though they include non-linguistic components such as arrows, traffic lights, fence barriers, etc. In order to exemplify their concept of the semiotic aggregate, the authors compare five street corners in Asia (Hong Kong and Beijing), Europe (Vienna and Paris), and the US (Washington, DC).

Scollon and Scollon (2003: 175–89) distinguish four main types of discourses in urban space: (1) municipal regulatory discourses, (2) municipal infrastructural discourses, (3) commercial discourses, and (4) transgressive discourses. Municipal regulatory and infrastructural discourses are signs produced by official organs. They include vehicular and pedestrian traffic signs, public notices, warnings and prohibitions, toponymic signs, inscriptions on utility poles, and others. All sorts of shop signs and other identifications of businesses are subsumed as commercial discourses. Transgressive discourses refer to signs that intentionally or accidentally violate the conventional semiotics expected in a certain place. The most prominent instance of this type of 'meaning out of place' (Scollon & Scollon, 2003: 161) is graffiti. The four types of signs form semiotic aggregates that, according to Scollon and Scollon, make all survey areas recognisable as urban street corners, some unmistakably distinctive features for each of the places notwithstanding.

The notion of the semiotic aggregate is but one part of Scollon and Scollon's overall approach to language on signs. The authors refer to this new field as 'geosemiotics', which they define as 'the study of the social meaning of the material placement of signs and discourses and of our actions in the material world' (Scollon & Scollon, 2003: 2). Geosemiotics consists of three components: the interaction order, visual semiotics, and place semiotics. Place semiotics is of central interest to the present study. It focuses on 'the ways in which the placement of discourse in the material world produces meanings that derive directly from that placement' (Scollon & Scollon, 2003: 22).

Place semiotics is divided into three parts: (1) code preference, (2) inscription, and (3) emplacement. Code preference deals with how signs represent the geopolitical world through the choice of languages, their graphic representation, and their arrangement if more than one language is contained on a sign. For instance, English signs imply an English-speaking community, Chinese signs a Chinese-speaking community, and so forth. However, this apparently straightforward relationship between the outside world and the language written on a sign does not always apply. One example discussed is a shop sign of a hairdresser in Nanjing, China, which reads 'Beauty Island'. The use of English in this case does not index any sizeable English-speaking community but rather serves 'to symbolize foreign taste and manners'. Thus, as Scollon and Scollon hold, the language on a sign 'can either index the community within which it is being used or can symbolize something about the product or business which has nothing to do with the place in which it is located' (2003: 119).

In distinguishing between indexical and symbolic meaning of language on signs, Scollon and Scollon make a similar point as Calvet (1990; see 3.5). Both see an indexical language use on a sign when there is a direct link between (graphic) speech signs and sign writer. Scollon and Scollon go one step further even in considering also those instances where the use of a language is intended to imply a relationship between language and sign writer that in reality doesn't seem to apply. The same strategy has been captured in the second part of Spolsky and Cooper's (1991; see 3.3) 'symbolic value' condition, which demands that you should 'write signs in a language with which you wish to be identified'.

Issues of code preference include the arrangement of two or more languages on a sign. As Scollon and Scollon point out, 'the mere fact that these items in a picture or in the world cannot be located simultaneously in the same place produces a choice system' (2003: 120). Based on a framework by Kress and van Leeuwen (1996), the authors determine a 'preferred code', which is to appear on top, on the left, or in the centre of a sign. A complementary 'marginalized code' is given on the bottom, on the right, or on the margins. These patterns can easily be observed in Hong Kong, where English until 1997 used to be placed in dominant position over Chinese on all official signs. The hierarchy of languages based on position can be cancelled by using different font sizes. An example given is a bilingual direction sign found in Killarney, Ireland. Though the Gaelic version appears on top, it is given in much smaller size than the English version below, suggesting that, despite its subordinate position, the latter is assigned greater prominence. Yet another option for code preference is the use of separate signs for each of the languages. In Ontario, Canada, for instance, traffic signs along the road may come in two versions, the English sign some metres ahead of the French one. The order of the languages is expressed in terms of coming into sight 'sooner' or 'later' (Scollon & Scollon, 2003: 119–28).

The second part of Scollon and Scollon's framework of place semiotics is inscription. The authors emphasise that different font types and orthographies carry different meanings. For instance, whether a text is written in simplified or in non-simplified Chinese characters makes a difference. In mainland China the 'new' simplified characters, according to Scollon and Scollon (2003: 130–3), are associated with the old political system of the socialist state. Paradoxically, visibility of the 'old' non-simplified set of characters as used in Hong Kong is described to be perceived of as an 'opening up to the outside world, to beauty parlors and karaoke lounges and to sex shops'.

Another issue subsumed under inscription is the material of a sign. Material conveys meaning with regard to properties such as permanence or durability, temporality or newness, and the quality of a sign. A text inscribed in a fixed, invariable way suggests greater authority than graffiti spray-painted on a wall. Characteristics like permanence and durability of a sign are indicated by the use of expensive materials, for instance marble engravings. Temporality and newness can also be indicated by what the authors refer to as 'layering', that is, attaching a sign to another sign in such a way that it appears more recent and more temporary than the sign it has been attached to.

The third part of Scollon and Scollon's framework of place semiotics is emplacement. It centres on the general space-dependency of signs. Holding that 'the geosemiotic meaning of a sign depends on where on earth it is placed', Scollon and Scollon (2003: 164) explore the indexical processes in which a space confers meaning on a sign. This point has already been discussed in section 2.1. Scollon and Scollon give the following example:

> In the case of a sign showing a lighted cigarette with a red circle and a slash we can read the universal slashed red circle to mean 'Do not smoke', but it is only by reference to a physical location that we know *where* to apply this restriction. The reading is based on where in space the sign is found. (2003: 164, emphasis original)

Scollon and Scollon's approach to language on signs highlights the interrelatedness of language and space and how they affect each other in the meaning-making process that is the linguistic landscape.

## 3.8 Rome: Approaches to the *Panorama Linguistico*

Rome is the capital of Italy, the seat of the Roman Catholic Church, and one of the world's most famous historic centres. The city has a population of around 2.5 million; the province of which it is part is home to almost four million people. The inhabitants of Rome since ancient times have been characterised by ethnic diversity. The present-day population according to official statistics includes an estimated 8% of people of non-Italian backgrounds from various parts of the world (Comune di Roma, 2005). Due to its numerous historic sites the Eternal City is also a magnet for international tourism, constantly attracting larger numbers of foreign travellers.

One aspect of Rome's linguistic landscape has been examined by Griffin (2004). He focused on the visual presence of English in the streets of the city. Griffin's paper is part of a series of related surveys with a similar research interest, all of which have recently been published in the journal *English Today*. They include smaller linguistic landscape accounts of Milan (Ross, 1997), Zurich, and Uppsala, Sweden (McArthur, 2000), three smaller central-European cities (Schlick, 2002), Tokyo (MacGregor, 2003), and some towns in north-western Portugal (Stewart & Fawcett, 2004). The basic aim of these surveys is to demonstrate how language on signs reflects a growing prominence of English in non-English-speaking locations around the world. That this phenomenon cannot solely be ascribed to the important role of English as an international language, but to a large extent results from the high prestige value of English worldwide, is the main tenor of these publications.

Griffin's study in Rome was conducted in summer 2003. It examines the use of English in 17 streets situated in seven distinct sections of the city that were previously selected on the map. All English words or phrases legible from arm's length were recorded on 'code sheets' and categorised with regard to the 'context' in which they appeared: on shop signs, either outside or in the shop window; on signs of public facilities like museums or monuments; on billboards, advertising posters or placards; etc. When English was used in combination with Italian, the Italian phrase was listed as well. Ten example photos per area were taken. Foreign languages other than English were not considered (Griffin, 2004: 5–6).

In total, 901 English words were recorded in 225 identified 'cases of English usage' in the 17 streets. They were most frequently found on commercial signs but were much less used on street signs or signs of public establishments. The fact that almost 75% of all cases of English usage contain four or fewer English words suggests that the conveyance of more complicated matters is generally left to Italian. While there are various examples of English texts addressing a non-Italian target group (e.g. 'English is spoken here', 'stamps available here'), English in many cases appears to be used as 'a device to establish a trendy cosmopolitan image to native Italian speakers' (e.g. 'Disco Moan', 'Universal Bar') (Griffin, 2004: 6–7). This finding is in line with most other *English Today* surveys. As Ross has observed:

> Any fleeting thoughts that these English signs are to be found because of the language's international role as a *lingua franca* or as an aid to international communication can surely be quashed without further ado. The simple reason for most of these shop signs is that English is today seen as an attractive and fashionable language. An English name lends an aura of chic prestige to a business, suggesting that it is part of the international scene, following the latest trends, up-to-date with the newest ideas ... Yes, English is important for communication world-wide, but English is also important because of the prestige associated with English-speaking countries, America in particular. (1997: 31)

While the prominence of English signs and their different types of target groups is a noticeable phenomenon in many places around the world, research exclusively focusing on this part of the linguistic land-scape runs the risk of missing another important factor involved in the making of a city's linguistic landscape: the languages of its non-indigenous population. In the case of Rome this newly developing multilingualism has been scrutinised in a larger research project by the

Italian Centre of Excellence for Research (Centro di Eccellenza della Ricerca) at the Siena University for Foreigners (Università per Stranieri di Siena).

One approach by the Centre aims at a systematic mapping of the *panorama linguistico* – the linguistic landscape. The Centre has developed a novel methodology for collecting linguistic landscape data using digital cameras and small handheld computers equipped with special software. All surveyed items upon being photographed are entered into a specially designed database and immediately geo-referenced with regard to their spatial position in an area. This procedure makes it possible to rapidly record larger amounts of data from which a precise, all-inclusive linguistic landscape map of a given territory can be designed. The methodology was first put into practice in Rome's Esquilino district – a neighbourhood in the historic centre of the city that in recent years has attracted increasingly large numbers of people with non-Italian backgrounds, particularly from Asian countries (Bagna & Barni, 2005, 2006).

First quantitative results of the Centre's research in the Esquilino district reveal a remarkably high visibility of languages other than Italian in this section of the city. The 849 collected signs contain no less than 23 languages. In addition, various instances of Italian with an unmistakably foreign impact were found, referred to as 'contact Italian' and counted separately. Further analysis of the data is based on a three-stage model focusing on (1) presence, (2) dominance, and (3) autonomy of the languages contained (see Table 3.6).

The presence of a language refers to its frequency of appearance on the 849 signs of the sample. Contained on 58.9% of all signs, Italian is represented most strongly. It is followed by Chinese (56.9%), English (32.6%), and Bengali (14.0%). All other languages are contained on less than 5% of the signs, with some of them included on one or two items only. The high frequency of Chinese and Bengali demonstrates how the Asian population of the Esquilino district has started to take hold of the area's linguistic landscape. Italian as the national language is comparatively weakly represented here (Bagna & Barni, 2006: 21–3).

The second category, dominance, analyses which of the languages contained on a sign is assigned the main part of the contents to be conveyed. As can be seen in Table 3.6, Chinese is the most important language on more than one-third of the signs. It is followed by Bengali (8.4%) and Italian (7.9%), only third in position in this category. Dominance could not be determined for 29% of the signs. The prominence of Chinese is also reflected by the third category, autonomy. Autonomous are those languages appearing without any other language on a sign. This applies to 296 items, two-thirds of which are Chinese signs. While English-only signs (11.1%) still have some quantitative relevance, all other languages, including Italian, only rarely appear alone

**Table 3.6** Languages on signs in Rome's Esquilino district

| (1) Presence | | | (2) Dominance | | | (3) Autonomy | | |
|---|---|---|---|---|---|---|---|---|
| *Language* | *n* | *%* | *Language* | *n* | *%* | *Language* | *n* | *%* |
| Italian | 500 | 58.9 | Chinese | 312 | 36.7 | Chinese | 197 | 66.6 |
| Chinese | 483 | 56.9 | Bengali | 71 | 8.4 | English | 33 | 11.1 |
| English | 277 | 32.6 | Italian | 67 | 7.9 | Bengali | 15 | 5.1 |
| Bengali | 119 | 14.0 | English | 55 | 6.5 | Italian | 15 | 5.1 |
| Singhalese | 32 | 3.8 | Singhalese | 29 | 3.4 | Russian | 9 | 3.0 |
| Spanish | 31 | 3.7 | Russian | 13 | 1.5 | 'Contact Italian' | 6 | 2.0 |
| Hindi | 24 | 2.8 | Spanish | 12 | 1.4 | Punjabi | 5 | 1.7 |
| French | 20 | 2.4 | 'Contact Italian' | 10 | 1.2 | Singhalese | 5 | 1.7 |
| Russian | 19 | 2.2 | Korean | 6 | 0.7 | Spanish | 3 | 1.0 |
| Arabic | 18 | 2.1 | Albanian | 5 | 0.6 | Arabic | 2 | 0.7 |
| 'Contact Italian' | 13 | 1.5 | Arabic | 5 | 0.6 | Korean | 2 | 0.7 |
| Rumanian | 13 | 1.5 | Punjabi | 5 | 0.6 | Albanian | 1 | 0.3 |
| German | 12 | 1.4 | Hindi | 3 | 0.4 | Japanese | 1 | 0.3 |
| Punjabi | 11 | 1.3 | Rumanian | 3 | 0.4 | Hindi | 1 | 0.3 |
| Korean | 10 | 1.2 | Japanese | 2 | 0.2 | German | 1 | 0.3 |
| Japanese | 10 | 1.2 | German | 2 | 0.2 | **Number of signs** | **296** | **100** |
| Albanian | 5 | 0.6 | French | 1 | 0.1 | | | |
| Tagalog | 4 | 0.5 | Tagalog | 1 | 0.1 | | | |
| Turkish | 2 | 0.2 | Ukrainian | 1 | 0.1 | | | |
| Persian | 1 | 0.1 | None | 246 | 29.0 | | | |
| Polish | 1 | 0.1 | **Number of signs** | **849** | **100** | | | |
| Portuguese | 1 | 0.1 | | | | | | |
| Ukrainian | 1 | 0.1 | | | | | | |
| Urdu | 1 | 0.1 | | | | | | |
| **Number of signs** | **849** | **100** | | | | | | |

*Source*: Bagna and Barni (2006: 21)

on a sign in the Esquilino district. Nine of the languages contained in the sample are used exclusively in combination with other languages (Bagna & Barni, 2006: 24–5).

In order to identify some distinctive combination patterns, the languages contained are categorised into five types: Italian, 'contact Italian', English, 'immigrant languages' (Chinese, Bengali, Singhalese, etc.), and 'others' (German, Japanese, etc.). The five language types combine into 15 patterns, the most frequent of which are 'immigrant language only' (28.4%), 'immigrant language + Italian' (24.3%), and 'immigrant language + English + Italian' (12.1%). Each of the 15 combinations is discussed and evaluated with regard to the number of language types included and its linguistic accessibility to potential sign readers (Bagna & Barni, 2006: 25–32).

The Centre's linguistic landscape approach to the Esquilino district thus goes far beyond a mere quantitative account of the languages contained. An analysis of the data based on the three-stage model shows that, although Italian is the language most frequently included on a sign (rank 1 in 'presence'), it is only rarely chosen to carry the main message (rank 3 in 'dominance'), and even less frequently appears without another language (rank 4 in 'autonomy'). These findings reveal a surprisingly weak position of the national language in this part of the Italian capital.

Two additional methodological tools complement the Centre's research. One focuses on spoken linguistic interaction in the streets, recording and mapping the number of participants involved, the direction of an exchange, and the type of interaction, among others. The other aims at demarcating 'closed' homogeneous spaces, such as ethnic businesses or foreigners' meeting places. The two additional analytical levels are to shed light on the question of what external factors are involved in determining the visibility of a given language in public space (Bagna & Barni, 2005: 343–9).

The two approaches to language on signs in Rome discussed in this section illustrate the overall width in scope of linguistic landscape research. They exemplify that differences in research interest and methodological effort may bring about completely different results, even in one and the same place. In combination, the two studies suggest that the salience of languages other than Italian in Rome is the result of two major trends: a growing visibility of the languages of the city's non-Italian population and a general proclivity towards the use of English on the part of the host society. Both points are important factors in shaping the linguistic landscape of the places discussed in the last two sections of this chapter, too.

## 3.9 Bangkok: Signs of Overt and Covert Language Policies

Bangkok is the capital of Thailand and its political, commercial, and cultural centre. Statistics about the total population of Bangkok give varying figures of between six and ten million people, depending on the underlying definition of the city's expanding boundaries. Most residents of Bangkok are native Thais, but the city is also home to a sizeable number of people of Chinese origin and various smaller linguistic minority groups from Asian and Western countries. Thailand's main language for international communication is English. It is a required school subject and enjoys high prestige value.

A general overview of the linguistic situation in Thailand is given by Smalley (1994). It includes a smaller survey of the capital's linguistic landscape. Smalley (1994: 203–6) focused on shop signs in three different parts of Bangkok: Charansanitwong Road, which runs through an area without sizeable linguistic minority groups; Yawarat Road, which is situated in a more Westernised section of the city; and Sukhumvit Road, which is part of an area with larger concentrations of Chinese residents. In each of the three locations the signs of 22 contiguous shops were surveyed. They were analysed with regard to the scripts displayed on each sign; the languages and scripts contained in the shop name on a sign; and the languages in which the services of a business were advertised.

The signs of Smalley's sample include three languages: Thai, Chinese, and English, which were represented in three scripts: Thai letters, Chinese characters, and the Roman alphabet. Their distribution shows some clear tendencies with regard to the three survey areas and their linguistic profiles. Concerning the overall visibility of the three scripts, for instance, signs containing Chinese characters and Roman letters were much more frequent on Yawarat Road and Sukhumvit Road, respectively, than on Charansanitwong Road. Nine out of ten signs on Yawarat Road contained Chinese writing, a proportion just as high as the share of signs with Roman letters found on Sukhumvit Road. On Charansanitwong Road, by contrast, less than one-third of the shop signs contained Chinese characters, and only 5% displayed Roman alphabet elements (Smalley, 1994: 203–4).

The same tendency was observable for the language in which a business advertised its services. While virtually no shops in the non-Chinese areas had signs announcing services in Chinese, 47% of the businesses in the Chinese section had such signs. Likewise, signs advertising services in English were scarce in the Thai section, but common in Sukhumvit Road, the section where most Westerners live (Smalley, 1994: 205).

Despite these clear trends concerning the geographic distribution of both languages and scripts, the relationship between the two itself was found to be far from straightforward. As a closer look at language- and script-mixing in the shop names displayed on the signs revealed, the choice of a language did not necessarily determine the script to be used. Thus, Thai script was found representing not only Thai language, but transliterated Chinese and English terms as well. Similarly, use of the Roman alphabet was not restricted to English terms, but was also used to represent terms of Chinese or Thai origin (Smalley, 1994: 205).

The languages and scripts of Bangkok's linguistic landscape have been given more attention in a recent study by Huebner (2006). It was conducted in July 2002 in 15 previously determined neighbourhoods in central and suburban Bangkok that were expected to adequately reflect the city's linguistic diversity. Each survey area was defined as one given stretch of the main street. In a few cases, for instance when the area was part of a shopping complex or a station, signs not representing a single street were included in the sample. The total number of items thus collected was 613. They were analysed with regard to their linguistic properties (scripts contained, combinations) and classified according to their 'source' as government related or non-related (Huebner, 2006: 34).

The main parts of Huebner's analysis are based on script rather than language, though he occasionally deviates from this principle. A total of 276 signs of the sample (45%) contain only one script, the residuary 337 signs (55%) two or more. The majority of the one-script signs were inscribed in the Thai or Roman alphabets. Other scripts occasionally found alone on a sign were Japanese, Arabic, and Chinese. The three most frequent script combinations were Thai–Roman, Thai–Roman–Chinese, and Thai–Chinese (Huebner, 2006: 38–9; see Table 3.7).

**Table 3.7** Government vs. non-government signs in Bangkok

| *Scripts contained:* | *Government signs (n = 101)* | *Non-government signs (n = 512)* | *Sum (n = 613)* |
|---|---|---|---|
| Thai | 59.4% | 19.1% | 25.8% |
| Roman | 3.0% | 20.1% | 17.3% |
| Thai/Roman | 33.7% | 33.0% | 33.1% |
| Thai/Roman/Chinese | 1.0% | 7.2% | 6.2% |
| Thai/Chinese | 1.0% | 3.1% | 2.8% |
| Others | 2.0% | 17.4% | 14.8% |
| **Total** | **100%** | **100%** | **100%** |

*Source*: Huebner (2006: 39)

An important analytical category in Huebner's study is the distinction between government and non-government signs. In a similar way to previous approaches to the topic (e.g. Ben-Rafael *et al.*, 2004, 2006; Calvet, 1990; Rosenbaum *et al.*, 1977) Huebner points out that official signs reflect the 'overt language policies of a given state', whereas items such as signs and advertisements of local businesses or notices posted by individuals are manifestations of the 'covert language policy of a community, and may display the grass roots cultural identity and aspiration of its members' (2006: 32).

A classification of the signs of the sample shows that government-related signs clearly constitute a minority, with only 16.5% of all signs. Most of them are either Thai-only or Thai–Roman signs, which according to Huebner (2006: 39) reflects 'the official Thai government policy of Thai as the official national language and English as the official language of wider communication internationally'. The occurrence of scripts other than Thai or Roman is virtually restricted to non-government signs, which show a linguistically much more diverse picture of the city. Table 3.7 juxtaposes the two types of signs and their linguistic properties.

Government-related signs exhibit little variation with regard to their geographic distribution across the 15 survey areas. The same cannot be said of the non-government signs, for which Huebner (2006: 40–7) identifies five distinctive geographic patterns: (1) areas dominated by Thai-only signs; (2) areas with predominantly Thai-only or Thai–English signs; (3) areas with high occurrences of Thai–Chinese signs; (4) areas in which Thai–English bilingual signs are the most frequent type of sign, and (5) areas with sizeable numbers of signs not containing Thai.

Discussing the five types of areas one by one, Huebner tries to recapture some of the diachronic developments of Bangkok's linguistic landscape. For instance, the fact that the areas dominated by Thai–Chinese signs hardly contain any Chinese-only signs can be taken as an indication of 'the Bangkok Chinese willingness to assimilate to Thai language and culture and the Thai willingness to incorporate them' (Huebner, 2006: 44). Another observation refers to a growing visibility of English as exemplified in the Thai–English bilingual areas. According to Huebner (2006: 44–6) each of the four areas represents a different stage in Bangkok's historical development. His data show that the frequency of English rises with perceived newness of an area. Taken together, these observations suggest a gradual shift from Chinese to English as Bangkok's language of wider communication.

A characteristic feature of Bangkok's linguistic landscape is Thai–English code-mixing. This frequently makes an unambiguous linguistic determination of a given text a highly problematic issue. Huebner (2006: 48–9) demonstrates that English influence on messages written in Thai is observable on various levels of linguistic analysis, including morphosyntax (branching direction), lexicon (borrowings), and orthography (use of spaces and periods between words). While elements of English can be frequently found in Thai-script texts, English texts in the Roman alphabet do not show any impacts of Thai. This non-reciprocal relationship, according to Huebner, is 'a function of access and equity' (2006: 48). It points to the fact that Roman alphabet texts address both a foreign and an educated Thai audience. Texts written in Thai script, on the other hand, are accessible to a Thai readership only, simply because most foreigners cannot read Thai. Inclusion of English elements in these messages is a strategy to add 'a cosmopolitan flair to the message that isn't available in a sign using only Thai script, lexicon and syntax' (Huebner, 2006: 48).

All in all, the survey by Huebner provides an instructive picture of Bangkok's linguistic diversity that significantly goes beyond the findings of Smalley's earlier approach. His account includes most major issues discussed in previous linguistic landscape research so far: discrepancies between official language policies and actual language usage, geographic distribution of languages and scripts, linguistic profiles of the sign readers, and problems of language and script contact, including linguistic mixing and changes in language preference patterns.

## 3.10 Tokyo: Reading Through the *Gengo Keikan*

Tokyo is the capital of Japan. It is a metropolitan prefecture divided into 23 wards, which constitute the central parts of Tokyo, 26 cities, 5 towns, and 8 villages. The total area of Tokyo covers 2187 square kilometres, with a population of over 12.3 million people (TMG, 2002, 2004a). Tokyo's non-Japanese population, according to official statistics, makes up around 2.9%, a ratio considerably lower than in most other world cities but considerably higher than the national average of 1.5% (MIC, 2004; TMG, 2004b). Over 80% of Tokyo's foreign residents come from Asian countries, mainly China and the Korean peninsula (see also 5.5).

Before discussing previous approaches to the linguistic landscape of Tokyo, it is necessary to give a brief outline of the Japanese writing system. Written Japanese is a combination of four scripts: Kanji, Hiragana, Katakana, and the 26 letters of the Roman alphabet. Kanji are Japanese adaptations of Chinese characters that are used to represent lexical morphemes. The number of Kanji to be used in official and daily correspondences is limited to fewer than 2000. It is common practice to add small side glosses called Furigana to difficult Kanji in order to indicate their reading.

Hiragana and Katakana are two indigenously developed syllabic scripts also referred to as Kana. Both Kana scripts consist of 48 syllable signs each. The main task of Hiragana is to represent grammatical morphemes and function words, while the Katakana script serves for emphasis, onomatopoetic expressions, and the transliteration of foreign words (other than Chinese, for which Kanji are used), among others. Roman letters, in Japan commonly referred to as *rōmaji*, are used for writing terms of foreign origin, acronyms, abbreviations, etc., and for the transliteration of Japanese terms. For the latter, two slightly different systems called Hepburn and Kunrei have coexisted to the present day.

Any longer passage of written Japanese is likely to contain all of the four scripts. The writing direction of Japanese texts traditionally runs from top to bottom on vertical lines shifting from right to left across the page. Nowadays, however, many Japanese texts are written in horizontal lines from left to right, in a similar way to most Western languages (Coulmas, 1996: 239–43).

In view of the complicated nature of the Japanese writing system, script choice has been an important issue in previous linguistic land-scape research in Tokyo. An early example is a survey by Masai (1972), a Japanese geographer who was among the first to use the term 'linguistic landscape' (*gengo keikan*) for this type of research. He examined language use on shop signs in the Shinjuku area, one of the centres of metropol-itan Tokyo. His sample consists of 3000 items collected in 1962. He analysed the names of the businesses given on these signs with regard to three parameters: (1) languages used, (2) scripts used, and (3) type of business.

The determination of the languages was based on etymological criteria. This had the somewhat unfavourable effect that even well-established Japanese borrowings were counted as non-Japanese. Masai classified 82% of the shop names as Japanese and 18% as non-Japanese. Foreign languages identified were English (9.8%), French (2.8%), Spanish (1.3%), Chinese (0.9%), German (0.8%), and Russian (0.6%), among others. With regard to the four scripts, Masai found that Kanji characters were most strongly represented. Names written exclusively in Kanji made up 42%, names combining Kanji with other scripts 77%. The representation of the other scripts and script combinations was as follows: only Hiragana 3%, Hiragana and others 20%; only Katakana 7%, Katakana and others 33%; and only Roman alphabet 3%, Roman alphabet and others 21% (Masai, 1972: 154–6). The data are summarised in Table 3.8.

Masai (1972: 156–7) also identified characteristic patterns of language choice for various types of businesses. The names of Japanese-style bars and other traditional Japanese establishments were almost completely made up of Japanese vocabulary. The Chinese items contained in Masai's sample appeared in names of Chinese restaurants. English names were mainly chosen for names of (non-foreign) restaurants and cafés. In general, Masai saw the use of foreign names in the commercial sector as a means to create an atmosphere of 'exoticism'. He held that the

**Table 3.8** Shop signs in central Tokyo

| Scripts | Frequency |
|---|---|
| Kanji only | 42% |
| Kanji contained | 77% |
| Hiragana only | 3% |
| Hiragana contained | 20% |
| Katakana only | 7% |
| Katakana contained | 33% |
| Roman alphabet only | 3% |
| Roman alphabet contained | 21% |

*Source*: Masai (1972: 155)

visibility of languages other than Japanese fulfilled a similar function to the import of American or European architecture to metropolitan Tokyo (Masai, 1972: 154).

A more recent survey with a similar scope was made by Someya (2002). She collected a sample of shop signs at 15 locations, mainly in areas around the stations of the Odakyū Line in the south-west of Tokyo. Between November 2001 and January 2002 she recorded around 1000 items by digital camera. Unlike Masai (1972), Someya's analysis included not only the shop names as given on the signs but commercial slogans and information about services and products as well. Not included were abbreviations like 'TEL' (telephone), 'F' (floor), or *'kabu'* (joint-stock company). Analytical parameters were script use and business type. Languages were not classified.

The quantitative results of Someya's analysis of script use on the signs of her sample are given in Table 3.9. Kanji is the script most frequently used, both in combination with others and standing alone. The two Kana scripts tend to appear mainly in combination with other scripts. The Roman alphabet is displayed on almost one-third of the sample items. On more than 10% it is the only script. It is used in order to represent both foreign and Japanese vocabulary (Someya, 2002: 222–5). In general, Someya's findings about script use show the same tendencies as Masai's earlier observations.

The use of Kanji was particularly frequent on signs of shops for matters of daily life. Other types of businesses tending to rely on Kanji were Chinese restaurants and Chinese pharmacies. Roman letters were preferably used in Western-style businesses like cafés or hairdressers, but also in domains concerning everyday life. They often appeared in mixed business names combining English common nouns with Japanese

**Table 3.9** Shop signs in south-western Tokyo

| Scripts | Frequency |
|---|---|
| Kanji only | 20% |
| Kanji contained | 75% |
| Hiragana only | 2% |
| Hiragana contained | 40% |
| Katakana only | 5% |
| Katakana contained | 39% |
| Roman alphabet only | 11% |
| Roman alphabet contained | 30% |

*Source*: Someya (2002: 223–4)

surnames. Examples are 'FRUITS YAOHIRO', 'CLEANING OZAWA', and 'Tominaga original Delicatessen', among others (Someya, 2002: 226).

Someya concludes her observations with a prognosis about the future development of Tokyo's linguistic landscape. She makes the following point:

> At present, the power of Kanji for writing on shop signs is still great. This trend is particularly strong for matters of everyday life. Yet, on the other hand, it is a fact that there is a surge of Roman letters. And rather than for writing Japanese words, it is used for writing foreign words. Whether doctors write the term *ganka* [ophthalmic clinic] as [the original English term] OPHTHALMOLOGY because they are aware of foreigners in Japan or if it is mere 'image writing' is not clear to me, but from now on this may well become a common way of writing.
>
> Recently, moreover, restaurants from overseas using signs with foreign scripts have appeared. Though some are aiming at an image effect for the Japanese public, many of these signs are addressed at foreigners staying in Japan. In some regions, particularly Chinese and Korean signs have become frequent. (Someya, 2002: 239–40)

Someya thus observes that the influx of the Roman alphabet and other scripts comes in conjunction with an influx of foreign languages. She sees two reasons for this development. On the one hand, the use of foreign languages gives a positive impression of a business to the Japanese public. This is a point frequently made in the literature on the topic (e.g. Haarmann, 1989; Loveday, 1996; Saint-Jacques, 1987; Takashi, 1992). On the other hand, signs in languages other than Japanese also serve the needs of a growing foreign population in Japan. In this sense, their appearance can be seen as an indication of increasing linguistic diversity on the societal level.

Questions concerning the target group of multilingual signs have also been dealt with in a linguistic landscape study by Inoue (2000: 16–20; also 1997: 47–50). However, unlike the two approaches discussed so far, Inoue concentrated on language rather than on script use. Working with a non-specified sample of mainly multilingual signs, he was particularly interested in the combinations in which the languages contained appeared on a sign. He identified 26 patterns, which are given in Table 3.10.

A look at the last column of Table 3.10 shows that Japanese and English are the only languages to appear alone on a sign (Nos. 7 and 25). All signs with two or more languages contain either Japanese or English. Signs with more than three languages tend to contain Chinese or Portuguese besides (only exception No. 16). As can be seen in the bottom line, the languages most frequently part of combinations are again English and Japanese. Each of them appears in 21 of the 26 patterns. They are followed by Chinese with 15, Korean, French, and Portuguese with 11, and Spanish with 10 cases.

Though not definable in quantitative terms, the combination patterns identified by Inoue are indicative of the high importance of English in Japan. As Inoue remarks, many of these signs, particularly when used in the commercial domain, address a Japanese rather than a foreign target group. On the other hand, the languages of both older (Chinese and Korean) and newer (Portuguese and Spanish) minorities appear on multilingual signs, too. Inoue holds that these types of multilingual signs do not aim at an 'image stimulation' by the Japanese population but have a predominantly foreign target group. The same motivations for foreign language use on signs have been identified by Someya (2002). Both currents contribute to the growing heterogeneity of Tokyo's linguistic landscape.

A linguistic landscape study with a completely different scope has been undertaken by the Tokyo Society for the Protection of Visually Disabled Persons' Lives and Rights (Tōshikyō, or *Tōkyō shiryoku shōgaisha no seikatsu to kenri o mamoru kai*). It focuses on Braille stickers and plates in public transportation. According to data by Tōshikyō (1994), an approximate number of 30,000 blind or visually disabled persons are living in the Tokyo metropolitan region. To these people, everyday problems with regard to language in public space have a more substantial character than for all other linguistic minority groups in Tokyo. As an earlier survey by Tōshikyō (1994) showed, 77% of all interviewed blind or visually disabled persons reported to have been injured one or several times while walking in the streets. At metro and railway stations, 50% had at least once had the experience of falling off the platform.

One major reason for the high number of platform accidents is lack of information about transfer, ticket gates, etc. Such information is usually

**Table 3.10** Combinations of languages on multilingual signs

| No. | IT | D | R | BE | U | A | IN | V | BU | S | G | PE | K | F | PO | TA | C | E | TW | TH | J | AI | Sum |
|---|---|---|---|---|---|---|---|---|---|---|---|---|---|---|---|---|---|---|---|---|---|---|---|
| 1 | 1 | | 1 | | | | | | | 1 | 1 | | 1 | 1 | | | 1 | 1 | | | | | 8 |
| 2 | | 1 | | | | | | | | 1 | 1 | | 1 | | | | 1 | 1 | | | | | 6 |
| 3 | | | | | 1 | | | | | | | | 1 | | | | 1 | 1 | | | | | 4 |
| 4 | | | | 1 | | 1 | | | | 1 | 1 | 1 | 1 | 1 | 1 | 1 | 1 | 1 | | | 1 | | 12 |
| 5 | | | | | | | | | | 1 | | | | | | | | 1 | | | | | 2 |
| 6 | | | | | | 1 | 1 | 1 | 1 | 1 | 1 | 1 | 1 | 1 | 1 | 1 | 1 | 1 | | 1 | 1 | | 15 |
| 7 | | | | | | | | | | | | | | | | | | 1 | | | | | 1 |
| 8 | | | 1 | | | | | | | 1 | | | 1 | 1 | 1 | | 1 | 1 | | | 1 | | 8 |
| 9 | | | | | | | | | | 1 | 1 | | 1 | 1 | 1 | | 1 | 1 | | | 1 | | 8 |
| 10 | | | | | | | | | | | 1 | | 1 | 1 | 1 | | | 1 | | | 1 | | 6 |
| 11 | | | | | | | | | | 1 | | | 1 | 1 | 1 | | 1 | 1 | 1 | 1 | 1 | | 9 |
| 12 | | | | | | | | | | | 1 | | | 1 | 1 | | 1 | 1 | | | 1 | | 6 |
| 13 | | | | | | | | | | 1 | | | | 1 | 1 | 1 | | 1 | 1 | 1 | 1 | | 8 |
| 14 | | | | | | | | | | | 1 | | 1 | | | | 1 | 1 | | | 1 | | 5 |
| 15 | | | | | | | | | | 1 | | | 1 | | | | 1 | 1 | | | 1 | | 5 |
| 16 | | | | | | | | | | | | | | | 1 | | 1 | 1 | | | 1 | | 4 |
| 17 | | | | | | | | | | | | | | | 1 | | 1 | 1 | | | 1 | | 4 |
| 18 | | | | | | | | | | | | 1 | | 1 | 1 | | | | | | 1 | | 4 |
| 19 | | | | | | | | | | | | | | 1 | | | 1 | 1 | | | 1 | | 4 |
| 20 | | | | | | | | | | | | | | | | | 1 | 1 | | 1 | 1 | | 4 |
| 21 | | | | | | | | | | | | | | | | | | 1 | | 1 | 1 | | 3 |
| 22 | | | | | | | | | | | 1 | | | | | | | | | | 1 | | 2 |
| 23 | | | | | | | | | | | | | | | | | | 1 | | | 1 | | 2 |
| 24 | | | | | | | | | | | | | | | | | | | | 1 | 1 | | 2 |
| 25 | | | | | | | | | | | | | | | | | | | | | 1 | | 1 |
| 26 | | | | | | | | | | | | | | | | | | | | | 1 | 1 | 2 |
| **Sum** | 1 | 1 | 2 | 1 | 1 | 2 | 1 | 1 | 1 | 10 | 9 | 3 | 11 | 11 | 11 | 3 | 15 | 21 | 2 | 6 | 21 | 1 | 135 |

*Notes*: IT=Italian, D=Dutch, R=Russian, BE=Bengali, U=Urdu, A=Arabic, IN=Indonesian, V=Vietnamese, BU=Burmese, S=Spanish, G=German, PE=Persian, K=Korean, F=French, PO=Portuguese, TA=Tagalog, C=Chinese, E=English, TW=Taiwanese (*sic*), TH=Thai, J=Japanese, AI=Ainu.

provided on small Braille plates attached to the handrails of the stairs. The basic principle is that the information given on one end of the stairs should be about the location at the other end of the stairs. In order to probe the quality of this system of information provision, Tōshikyō (2000) conducted a survey of the 29 stations of the Yamanote Line, a circle railway line through the centre of Tokyo. Data were collected between July 1999 and March 2000. A total of 712 plates were examined. These were evaluated on an eight-tiered scale containing the following categories: (1) no Braille available, (2) unreadable/hard to read, (3) incorrect information, (4) insufficient information, (5) plate inappropriately positioned, (6) any other problem concerning the plate, (7) others, and (8) no problems. If more than one of the first seven problems was found, the plate was subsumed under the category of the highest order.

The results of the survey reveal that the situation for people relying on Braille when using public transport is far from satisfactory. Only 432 items (61%) were considered adequate. No fewer than 280 items (39%) showed at least one of the above-mentioned deficiencies, while 135 items (19%) of these pertain to one of the first three categories with particularly severe deficiencies. Barely five of the 29 Yamanote Line stations did not use any plates classified under categories one to seven, while plates with at least one deficiency of the first three categories were found at more than half of the stations (Tōshikyō, 2000: 1–5). The basic data are given in Table 3.11.

**Table 3.11** Braille plates at railway stations in central Tokyo

| Category | 1 | 2 | 3 | 4 | 5 | 6 | 7 | 8 | Total |
|---|---|---|---|---|---|---|---|---|---|
| Frequency | 4% | 10% | 4% | 10% | 6% | 2% | 2% | 61% | 100% |

*Source*: Tōshikyō (2000: 3)

In summary, previous research into the linguistic landscape of Tokyo has shown that the streets of the city are a place of written language contact. Though Japanese is predominant, the signs of the city bring together a variety of languages and scripts other than Japanese, intended to serve both foreign and Japanese groups of the population in differing but not always clearly distinguishable ways. It also becomes obvious that most of the more recent analytical categories developed in linguistic landscape research so far have not been applied to Tokyo.

The next chapter gives a summary of the major issues dealt with in previous research and integrates them into an overall framework for the study of the linguistic landscape. This framework will be put into practice in Chapter 5.

## Chapter 4
# *Summary*

This chapter summarises the main findings made in previous research and draws some overall conclusions. We start with a few general remarks about linguistic landscape research, the development of the field, and its basic preoccupations so far. The main problems pertaining to language on signs as examined in previous research can be captured in the following three questions:

(1)  Linguistic landscaping by whom?
(2)  Linguistic landscaping for whom?
(3)  Linguistic landscape *quo vadis*?

Discussing these questions one by one, a general framework for the study of language on signs will be outlined, the applicability of which will be demonstrated in the following chapter. The closing section discusses the methodological problems concerning empirical research into language on signs. It emphasises that the development of a sound methodology of data collection will be vital for the future development of the discipline.

## 4.1 General Observations

The overview of previous research in Chapter 3 has shown that some pioneer linguistic landscape studies had been conducted decades before Landry and Bourhis in 1997 finally 'invented' the discipline by providing it with a proper name. Though the term itself already had been occasionally used in previous research in French (Monnier, 1989; see 3.2) and Japanese (Masai, 1972; see 3.10), most of the approaches available so far must be considered linguistic landscape research *avant la lettre*. In fact, only four of the examples discussed in the previous chapter make direct reference to Landry and Bourhis: Bagna and Barni (2005, 2006; see 3.8), Ben-Rafael *et al.* (2004, 2006; see 3.3), Cenoz and Gorter (2006; see 3.4), and Huebner (2006; see 3.9).

An important external factor for the development of the discipline has been the spread of digital cameras. As Gorter (2006: 2) has remarked, the introduction of this technological novelty offering 'sufficient memory for a reasonable price allows researchers to take an apparently unlimited number of pictures of the signs in the linguistic landscape'. In this respect it must be kept in mind that the pioneers of linguistic landscape research with regard to data collection were faced with problems incomparably more serious than researchers today. They either had to make do with analogue photos (e.g. Calvet, 1990, 1994; Spolsky & Cooper, 1991) – a procedure not only more costly but also less reliable concerning the eventual usability of a recorded item – or wholly rely on notes taken during their research out in the streets (e.g. Rosenbaum *et al.*, 1977; Tulp, 1978).

The emergence only recently of something like a coherent discipline is likely to have benefited much from technological developments. In a certain sense, the spread of digital cameras around the turn of the century has been of similar importance to the study of the linguistic landscape as was the diffusion and availability of portable tape-recorders back in the 1960s to Labovian research (see Joseph *et al.*, 2001: 145). Table 4.1 enlists all examples of previous research mentioned or discussed in the present study in chronological order.

As explored in Chapter 2, language on signs is a form of impersonal communication via written messages attached to immovable carriers in public space. These messages make up a vital part of information provision in urban everyday life. A city without signs would be more than inconvenient – it would be largely unintelligible. However, previous research into language on signs has emphasised that there is more to the use of written language in public space than providing information by way of graphic speech signs. The linguistic landscape is the focal point of two of the most essential markers of ethnic identity, language and place. Writing one's language on a sign is a means of marking the territory (Calvet, 1990: 75) – of declaring power over space (Spolsky & Cooper, 1991: 84). In other words, 'there is no more obvious way for a group to assert its existence than by putting up billboards' (Coulmas, 2005: 207). The indexicality of language on public signs thus not only refers to the meaning that a space confers on a sign – a point discussed in sections 2.1 and 2.2, but the same relationship applies the other way round, too: a sign confers meaning on a space. In this sense, the visibility or non-visibility of a language in public is a message of and in itself.

One major theme that links most previous approaches to language on signs is globalisation and its impacts on local linguistic ecologies. Large-scale migration movements, calls for political participation, and the power of global market forces are among the main factors increasingly affecting the complex relationships between the languages of minority communities, the national or official language(s), and English as the one global language of our times (Coulmas & Heinrich, 2005). The linguistic

**Table 4.1** Previous linguistic landscape studies: Chronological overview

| Year | Survey | Section no., this volume |
|------|--------|--------------------------|
| 1960–9 | Masai, 1972 | 3.10 |
| 1970–9 | Rosenbaum *et al.*, 1977 | 3.3 |
|  | Tulp, 1978 | 3.1 |
| 1980–9 | Calvet, 1990, 1994 | 3.5 |
|  | Monnier, 1989 | 3.2 |
|  | Spolsky & Cooper, 1991 | 3.3 |
| 1990–4 | Smalley, 1994 | 3.9 |
|  | Wenzel, 1996 | 3.1 |
| 1995–9 | CLF, 2000 | 3.2 |
|  | Inoue, 2000 | 3.10 |
|  | McArthur, 2000 | 3.8 |
|  | Ross, 1997 | 3.8 |
|  | Tōshikyō, 2000 | 3.10 |
| 2000+ | Bagna & Barni, 2005, 2006 | 3.8 |
|  | Ben-Rafael *et al.*, 2004, 2006 | 3.3 |
|  | Cenoz & Gorter, 2006 | 3.4 |
|  | Griffin, 2004 | 3.8 |
|  | Huebner, 2006 | 3.9 |
|  | Itagi & Singh, 2002a | 2.3 |
|  | Kim, 2003, 2004 | 5.5 |
|  | MacGregor, 2003 | 3.8 |
|  | Reh, 2004 | 3.6 |
|  | Schlick, 2002 | 3.8 |
|  | Scollon & Scollon, 2003 | 3.7 |
|  | Someya, 2002 | 3.10 |
|  | Stewart & Fawcett, 2004 | 3.8 |

landscape can be read as a reflection of the complicated interplay between these languages and their differing social standings.

As the increasing body of linguistic landscape research worldwide reveals, both indigenous and non-indigenous linguistic minorities make themselves visible by writing their languages on the walls of the city. We see Basque signs in Donosita, Wolof signs in Dakar, and Arabic signs in Jerusalem, but likewise read Chinese in the streets of Bangkok, Paris, and Rome. Owing to both its wide communicative range and its high prestige value worldwide, English is the language omnipresent in virtually all of the linguistic landscapes, irrespective of whether or not it is actually spoken by any sizeable share of the population. English signs, with and without local impact, are as common in Beijing and Brussels as they are in Lira and Ljouwert.

Despite strong differences with regard to place of observation, applied methodology, and underlying research perspective, three basic questions informing the study of the linguistic landscape can be identified. They refer to the writers, the readers, and the diachronic development of language in public space, respectively:

(1) Linguistic landscaping by whom?
(2) Linguistic landscaping for whom?
(3) Linguistic landscape *quo vadis*?

Let us now discuss these questions in detail.

## 4.2 Linguistic Landscaping By Whom?

The first question refers to the originator or source of a sign. The most basic distinction here is between official and non-official items. For instance, Scollon and Scollon (2003) subdivide a city's 'semiotic aggregate' into municipal signs on one hand and commercial (and transgressive) signs on the other; Calvet (1990, 1994) distinguishes between government related 'in vitro' and government non-related 'in vivo' items; and Ben-Rafael *et al.* (2004, 2006) classify their survey items into 'top-down' and 'bottom-up' signs. As Calvet's research in Dakar has shown, this distinction contains hints as to both the linguistic make-up of the population and the readiness of official agents to acknowledge the situation. The same point has been made for Jerusalem by Rosenbaum *et al.* (1977) and for Bangkok by Huebner (2006). Official language policies may also account for the order of the languages on a sign. Examples are Montreal (3.2), Jerusalem (3.3), and Hong Kong (3.7). Scollon and Scollon (2003) have referred to this expression of unequal power relations between coexisting linguistic groups as 'code preference'.

A next point concerning the provision of public signs is regularities with regard to the geographic distribution of the languages. Such regularities have been conspicuous in Brussels (3.1) and Montreal (3.2), where the visibility of a language corresponds to the spatial distribution of the two major linguistic groups of the city. Similarly, the special ethnolinguistic population make-up of East Jerusalem has been identified to account for characteristics in its linguistic landscape that clearly deviate from those in the western parts of the city (3.3). Concentrations of signs containing non-alphabet scripts in the Belleville area of Paris are an example of how the linguistic landscape indicates non-indigenous populations within the city. Calvet (1994) in this respect has observed how some ethnolinguistic groups make their presence felt visually more than others.

The relationship between the linguistic properties of a sign and the linguistic background of the sign writer is another major point discussed in previous research. In Montreal, for instance, Monnier (1989) found that the language on the signs outside a shop predicts the language in which one will be served inside. A related case is Calvet's (1990) example of Chinese shop signs in Paris. However, the main function of the language here is to index the Chinese background of the business. It is irrelevant that the majority of Parisian passers-by are unable to make sense of the characters on the sign. Previous studies have further identified cases where no direct relationship between language use and the sign writer's linguistic background applies. Scollon and Scollon (2003) refer to such instances as symbolic rather than indexical language use. It needs to be re-emphasised that indexicality is a quality that applies to all signs in relating them to the circumstances of their emplacement (see 2.1). Thus, on a higher level, symbolic language use has indexical properties as well. It indexes a preference for foreign language use by the non-foreign population, which is a point of special relevance with regard to the worldwide spread of English signs.

A final aspect concerning the source of a sign is the relationship between commercial domain and the languages contained. In Lira Town, for instance, Reh has observed various regularities in the distribution of Lwo and English with regard to the type of business in which a sign was used. The fact that virtually all previous surveys find some similar correlations suggests that commercial domain is an important variable in determining the languages to be used on a sign.

## 4.3 Linguistic Landscaping For Whom?

Our second question concerns the readers of the signs. According to Spolsky and Cooper's (1991) framework, the 'presumed reader' condition is one of the key determinants for a language to be displayed in public space. A major problem is what linguistic groups of the population the languages on a sign are supposed to serve. Previous research has shown that signs containing foreign languages do not necessarily have a foreign target group. In Tokyo as a particularly striking example, the use of foreign languages for a mainly Japanese readership has been described in terms such as 'exoticism' (Masai, 1972), 'image writing' (Someya, 2002), or 'image stimulation' (Inoue, 2000). The desire of a by and large monolingual population for multilingual signs appears to be an important aspect in determining the linguistic landscape, in Tokyo as elsewhere.

An important point is the linguistic profile of the recipients of the signs. For all cases in which Spolsky and Cooper's 'presumed reader' condition applies, a multilingual sign contains information about the linguistic profile of the population, both on the societal and on the individual level. Reh's (2004) categorisation of multilingual signs into duplicating, fragmentary, overlapping, and complementary multilingual writing identifies different underlying expectations of the linguistic proficiency of the sign readers. For instance, the functional arrangement of English and Lwo on bilingual signs in Lira Town presupposes a bilingual reader, because the two languages do not constitute mutual translations but give separate contents. The fact that the Lwo part of the signs is linguistically more complex implies that individual language proficiency is higher in Lwo than in English. Local characteristics of arranging information on multilingual signs thus allow for various conclusions about a population's linguistic status quo.

A second point concerning the targeted readership of multilingual signs is desired visibility or non-visibility of a sign's multilingual nature. Reflecting a population's general attitudes towards their city's linguistic landscape, this question is particularly important in bilingual environments. In Brussels, for instance, the co-appearance of French and Dutch on the same sign is rare (Wenzel, 1996). As mentioned in section 3.1, it is safe to interpret this strict separation of the two languages as an expression of continuing linguistic conflict between Brussels' two major linguistic groups. Judging from the studies available so far, there is a paradoxical tendency for multilingual cities to long for a monolingual landscape, while the inhabitants of a by and large monolingual city favour visibly multilingual signs. In other words, foreign languages are fine as long as they come without any sizeable group of speakers.

## 4.4 Linguistic Landscape *Quo Vadis*?

The third question concerns the dynamics of languages and scripts in contact. It focuses on what the signs out in the streets reveal about the diachronic development of a city's linguistic condition. Written language is a congenial research object in this respect, because it visualises the instability of language contact situations. One point frequently discussed is language- and script-mixing. A good example is the representation of foreign vocabulary in Lira Town, where Reh (2004) has observed some English terms being given in original spelling while others appear as loan words in Lwo orthography. The flux of the situation gets even more pronounced when more than one script is involved and when different options for the graphic representation of a message on a sign are at hand. One example is the linguistic landscape of Dakar, where Calvet (1990, 1994) has observed various alternatives for writing Wolof and

Arabic texts. Availability of more than one script in order to graphically represent a message is an issue in the case of Tokyo, too.

A second point concerning the diachronic perspective is a change in language preference patterns. The comparative studies conducted in Brussels (3.1) and Montreal (3.2) both suggest an increase of English at the expense of the other languages involved. This tendency is observed both where English is one of the major languages concurring (Montreal) and where it is not (Brussels). The language of the signs here clearly reflects the increasing power of English in a globalising world. An alternative method of examining the diachronic development of the linguistic landscape is Spolsky and Cooper's (1991) focus on coexisting older and newer versions of a given type of sign. The advantage of this approach is that it is applicable also when data from only one point in time are at hand.

The three questions cover all major points dealt with in linguistic landscape research so far. They are intended to provide a first tentative frame to the study of language on signs. Before applying this frame in practice in the next chapter, some methodological problems concerning LL research need to be addressed.

## 4.5 Methodological Issues

In order to summarise the main methodological problems, let us first make a basic distinction between qualitative and quantitative approaches. Examples of the former type are Calvet (1990, 1994), Reh (2004), and Scollon and Scollon (2003). Their surveys contain important observations about language use on signs regarding issues such as discrepancies between official language policies and everyday linguistic practices; different formats of multilingual messages and their implications with regard to the linguistic profile of the population; problems of language and script contact; indexical and symbolic functions of language on signs; and the overall significance of the linguistic landscape for the semiotic construction of the public space. Qualitative approaches generally show little interest in clearly defining the corpus of items their analysis is based on, which is fine as long as a quantitative evaluation of the data is avoided. It is rather dubious, however, to observe trends such as 'a *considerable* increase in the amount of Japanese writing' in Hong Kong (Scollon & Scollon, 2003: 133, my emphasis) in the absence of quantitative data to confirm this assessment.

Approaches mainly quantitative in scope are Tulp (1978), Wenzel (1996), Monnier (1989), and the Council of the French Language (CLF, 2000), among others. They work with a clearly defined and systematically collected sample of signs, because their chief aim is to ascertain the representative strength of the languages on public display. Analytical categories other than the language or languages contained are not, or only sporadically, considered. Most of the more recent approaches aim at combining a sound methodology of data collection with various types of qualitative analyses. Good examples are Ben-Rafael *et al.* (2004, 2006), Cenoz and Gorter (2006), and Huebner (2006).

Collecting a sample of signs involves three main problems. It must be clarified how to determine (1) the survey area(s), (2) the survey items, and (3) their linguistic properties. For the geographic determination of survey areas it has proved helpful to make use of roads or railway lines as orientation markers (Rosenbaum *et al.*, 1977; Someya, 2002; Tōshikyō, 2000; Tulp, 1978; Wenzel, 1996). Another option is delineating survey areas by street blocks, as done by the Centre of Excellence for Research in Rome's Esquilino district (Bagna & Barni, 2005, 2006). A sophisticated way of defining arbitrarily determined survey areas has been developed by the Council of the French Language in Montreal (CLF, 2000). To be clarified is how representative of a city as a whole the survey areas should be, and how representative of a survey area as a whole the collected signs should be. This latter point refers to the question of whether all or only some of the signs found in a given area should be included in the sample, which brings us to the second problem.

Of fundamental importance to all data-driven approaches is the question of what constitutes the 'unit of analysis' (Gorter, 2006: 3). Some previous studies include newspapers, books, and other printed matters into their corpora (Reh, 2004; see also Hannahs, 1989); others complement their research by additional data on spoken language (Bagna & Barni, 2005; Monnier, 1989; Rosenbaum *et al.*, 1977). While such supplementary levels of analysis will no doubt yield interesting insights, it should be re-emphasised that the term 'linguistic landscape' itself should not be expanded beyond the definition given by Landry and Bourhis (1997), that is, language written on signs. The question is what type of signs.

The survey items of many quantitative approaches are confined to signs of a commercial nature, such as shop signs (CLF, 2000; Masai, 1972; Monnier, 1989; Rosenbaum *et al.*, 1977; Smalley, 1994; Someya, 2002) or advertisement billboards (Tulp, 1978; Wenzel, 1996). It may be helpful to concentrate on such clearly definable entities because this simplifies the procedure of data collection and a comparison of the results. On the other hand, many aspects of a city's linguistic landscape are not captured when focusing on one type of sign only. In this respect, qualitatively oriented studies such as Calvet (1990, 1994), Scollon and Scollon (2003), or Spolsky and Cooper (1991) have a much wider scope, including both official and non-official, and both commercial and non-commercial signs.

When counting the survey items, two alternative approaches are feasible. One can define each sign as one item or work with semantic rather than physical entities such as 'information units' (Monnier, 1989), 'messages' (CLF, 2000), or 'cases' (Griffin, 2004). A semantic definition is bound to run into unclear cases, but the physical determination of the boundaries of a sign is a tricky problem, too. Questions such as whether the front and the backside of a sign constitute one or two items (Tulp, 1978: 276) or how to deal with defaced signs (Spolsky & Cooper, 1991: 89) and other forms of 'denied inscriptions' (Scollon & Scollon, 2003: 138) must be clarified in advance if a sound methodology of data collection is to be guaranteed. In how far it may be reasonable to summarise all signs used by a given establishment into one larger 'unit of analysis', as practised by Cenoz and Gorter (2006), is another question to be considered.

The third major problem is how to categorise the survey items in linguistic terms. A distinction between translation and transliteration as made by Spolsky and Cooper (1991) will help solve many, though not all, problems of classification. If two or more scripts are in regular use, one can base the determination of the languages on the choice of the scripts. An example is Rosenbaum *et al.*'s (1977) survey of Jerusalem, where script rather than language is taken as the defining criterion. A similar approach is taken by Smalley (1994) and Huebner (2006) for their research in Bangkok. That the graphic representation is an important issue in the case of Tokyo, too, is evident from the fact that it is included as a variable in the surveys by Masai (1972) and Someya (2002). However, the relationship between language and script is complicated and does not allow for a linguistic determination based on script choice alone. Both language and script need to be taken into account.

As has been pointed out, a strong proclivity towards the use of English, especially in the commercial domain, has been observed in virtually all research environments. As a result, the frequency of multilingual signs would vary considerably according to whether or not one decides to count signs with English names of shops, companies, products, brands, etc. as signs containing English. Wenzel (1996) has formulated some general principles concerning the counting of English phrases, while Monnier (1989) and the Council of the French Language (CLF, 2000) have excluded all proper names from their surveys. It is no doubt important to have clearly defined regulations as to the counting of English-looking terms. Yet it is problematic to ignore English names and slogans in total, because the general proclivity towards English in itself has something to say, too, about the linguistic landscape of a place.

These are some of the basic methodological problems involved in the empirical study of language on signs. In closing, it should be emphasised that a sound methodology is highly important if the study of the linguistic landscape is to become a serious sociolinguistic research tool. Walking through the streets and taking photos of anything that might strike one as particularly curious, illustrative, or, worse still, 'representative' is unlikely to yield any scientifically relevant results. While this has been common sense in sociolinguistic research on spoken language for decades, much remains to be done when it comes to empirical research into written language.

# Chapter 5
## Case Study: Signs of Multilingualism in Tokyo

Having introduced a basic frame for the study of the linguistic landscape, this chapter is dedicated to applying this frame to a real corpus of signs. We will focus on a sample of multilingual signs recently collected in the streets of Tokyo. It will be shown that these signs in a wider sense can be read as signs of a nascent multilingualism within Japanese society.

That Japan is commonly quoted as one of the prototypes of a monolingual nation is a by-product of the modernisation process starting in the second half of the 19th century (Carroll, 2001; Lee, 1996). While national language policies and monolingual ideology in the past two centuries succeeded in eliminating much of the archipelago's former linguistic heterogeneity, a growing influx of people who speak a language other than Japanese in recent years has entailed trends of a new linguistic diversification. These developments have brought about new perspectives on 'multiethnic Japan' (Lie, 2001), 'multicultural Japan' (Denoon et al., 1996; also Douglass & Roberts, 2000), and 'multilingual Japan' (Maher & Yashiro, 1995; also Coulmas & Heinrich, 2005; Goebel Noguchi & Fotos, 2001).

How does the linguistic landscape of Tokyo reflect these trends? Who is involved in the making of Tokyo's multilingualism, who is supposed to profit from it, and what direction does it take? As shall be demonstrated, a look at the signs of the city provides various empirically derived insights about increasing linguistic diversity in the Japanese capital. We start with a few methodological remarks about the design of the survey and its basic quantitative results. Subsequent sections discuss the following nine analytical categories: languages contained (5.2) and combinations (5.3); official and non-official signs (5.4); regularities in geographic distribution (5.5); availability of translation or transliteration (5.6); visual prominence (5.7); visibility of a sign's multilingual nature (5.8); linguistic idiosyncrasies (5.9); and coexistence of older and newer signs (5.10). The main findings will be summarised in the concluding chapter.

**Table 5.1** Research questions and analytical categories

| Research questions | Analytical categories |
|---|---|
| All | Languages contained (5.2) |
| | Combinations (5.3) |
| Linguistic landscaping by whom? | Top-down vs. bottom-up (5.4) |
| | Geographic distribution (5.5) |
| | Code preference (5.7) |
| Linguistic landscaping for whom? | Part writing (5.6) |
| | Visibility (5.8) |
| Linguistic landscape *quo vadis*? | Idiosyncrasies (5.9) |
| | Layering (5.10) |

An analysis of the languages contained and how they are combined on the signs of the sample is of relevance with regard to all of the three research questions: the sign writers, the sign readers, and the language contact situation as a whole. The other categories to be discussed predominantly focus on one of the three points each. Sections 5.4, 5.5, and 5.7 deal with the question of who contributes to the making of the linguistic landscape, sections 5.6 and 5.8 address the problem of whom it is to serve, and sections 5.9 and 5.10 touch on diachronic issues. The relationship between the three research questions and the nine categories is sketched in Table 5.1.

## 5.1 Methodology and Basic Results

According to the three points about data collection outlined in section 4.5, the methodology of the present survey is based on the following steps: (1) the determination of the survey areas, (2) the determination of countable items, and (3) the distinction between monolingual and multilingual signs. They will be discussed in turn.

### Spatial determination of the survey areas

As geographic orientation marker I selected the 29 stations of the Yamanote Line, a circular railway line connecting Tokyo's major city centres. The 34.5 km tour around the whole circle takes around 60 minutes, within which one gets to see a variety of sites in 10 of Tokyo's 23 wards. Though many of the stations are situated in crowded business, shopping, or entertainment districts, there are also less busy areas, quiet residential neighbourhoods, and parks. The environments of the 29

Yamanote Line stations thus provide a multilayered picture of the centre of the city.

Each survey area was part of a street between two consecutive traffic lights previously selected on the map (see Appendix on p. 147–8). It had to be inside the loop described by the Yamanote Line and if possible run more or less at a right angle from the rails to the centre. It should not be too far off the station, but the station entrance area itself was avoided because in many cases there is a square area that is hard to define in spatial terms. I had not been familiar with most of the places. The advantage of this selection principle was that it guaranteed a unified and non-biased determination of survey areas. A disadvantage was that the distances between the traffic lights varied strongly from approximately 65 metres in the survey area in Okachimachi to 400 metres in the survey area in Shinagawa. The mean distance is 154 metres. Another problem was that, in one case, Nippori, there were no traffic lights in the vicinity of the station from inside the loop and hence no survey area could be determined. This reduced the number of areas to 28.

Each survey area was enclosed by the traffic lights of two consecutive intersections or junctions. The end points of an area were the traffic light poles closest together in length, including pedestrian lights. In breadth, the limits of the survey areas were defined by spatial boundaries on both sides of the street, in most cases buildings. Cross streets were not considered part of the survey area. A major problem was larger spaces like parks or gardens, parking lots, and roofed malls along the street. They were excluded as far as possible, but in some cases I had to rely on ad hoc decisions. In height, no special limitations needed to be made. In some cases a few signs appeared to be hard to decipher, but most of the signs were legible from street level without major problems. The majority of all signs were put up within three or four metres off the ground.

### Counting the items

A sign was considered to be any piece of written text within a spatially definable frame. The underlying definition is physical, not semantic. It is rather broad, including anything from the small handwritten sticker attached to a lamp-post to huge commercial billboards outside a department store. Items such as 'push' and 'pull' stickers at entrance doors, lettered foot mats, or botanic explanation plates on trees were considered signs, too. The object to which a sign is attached (a shop window, a door, a building, etc.) will be called the carrier. The carrier may be identical with the sign (a traffic sign, a standing signboard in front of a shop, etc.), that is, a space created with the sole purpose of displaying a text. A carrier can provide more than one surface for display (e.g. the front and the backside of a flag, the sides and the top of a fire extinguisher box), in which case each lettered side was considered to be a separate item.

Each sign contained in one of the 28 survey areas was counted as one item, irrespective of its size. Excluded were texts directly written on products, price tags attached to them, as well as signs inside shops or behind the shop windows unless attached to or in direct proximity to the window pane. The same rule applied to telephone boxes and cigarette vending machines. Other sorts of signs excluded were small tags on vending machines of 'hot' and 'cold' drinks. All non-stationary objects were ignored, too. This refers particularly to printed materials like newspapers and journals or price lists and menus for takeaway, but also to texts written on vehicles (buses, cars, etc.), clothes (T-shirts, baseball caps, etc.), as well as tattoos and the like. Yet another sort of signs not counted were items without text, such as pictures, emblems, logos, and pictograms.

Since there were no other limitations than those just described, the items counted in some of the locations were quite numerous. In the 190-metre survey area in Akihabara, for instance, I found no fewer than 1054 items, many of them smaller than DIN A4 size. Several counting alternatives such as a limitation of countable items based on a minimum size or an arbitrary numerical determination (e.g. count at most 20 items per building) had been considered. Eventually they were rejected in favour of the count-all procedure, which, though not very sophisticated, turned out to be least problematic from a methodological point of view.

### Monolingual vs. multilingual

All countable items were categorised as either mono- or multilingual. A multilingual sign was determined to be a sign (as defined above) sharing one or either of the following characteristics: (1) containing at least one language in addition to, or instead of, Japanese; or (2) containing Japanese represented in Roman alphabet, Japanese supplemented by Furigana annotations, or Japanese in Braille (see 3.10). Both parts of the definition yield a certain number of multilingual signs that actually contain only one language – Japanese or other. It was considered necessary to work within such a broad frame in order not to miss relevant parts of Tokyo's linguistic landscape. However, it should be kept in mind that the term 'multilingual' henceforth is used for the sake of terminological simplicity rather than with strict correspondence to a multiplicity of languages.

The second part of the definition was uncomplicated. It suffices to add that Braille does not include textured pavement blocks, which have become a frequent sight in the streets of Japanese cities (for details see

MLIT/JICE, 2003: 219–36). The first part of the definition involved more difficulties. The main problem was to decide whether or not the text on a sign was recognisable as a language other than Japanese. As shown in section 3.10, use of foreign vocabulary, especially English, has high prestige value in Japan. The result is a considerable degree of language contact between Japanese and English (Haarmann, 1989; Honna, 1995; Loveday, 1996; Stanlaw, 2004), known to be particularly prominent in the commercial sector (Saint-Jacques, 1987; Takashi, 1992). The streets of Tokyo are overflowing with commercial signs and billboards containing English words and phrases.

Since it proved impracticable to categorise the data on the basis of linguistic aspects alone, some default rules were formulated for dealing with unclear cases. It was determined that anything written in Japanese Kanji characters or the two indigenous Kana syllabaries (see 3.10) was counted as Japanese. Even if the Roman alphabet was used, this was not considered a sufficient requirement to identify a language other than Japanese in the following cases: (1) international measure units and abbreviations like 'm' (metre), 'F' (floor), 'P' (parking), 'S'/'M'/'L' (small, medium, large), 'tel', 'am'/'pm', etc.; (2) computer nomenclature, www pages, and e-mail addresses; (3) language on credit card stickers; (4) single words within coherent Japanese text; and (5) names of companies and brands, including acronyms ('Gucci', 'NTT Docomo', etc.) unless containing information about the nature of the business. Use of the Roman alphabet was considered relevant to categorise a sign as multi-lingual in the following cases: (1) single words or phrases not embedded into Japanese text; and (2) names of companies or brands that do contain information about the nature of the business ('Resona Bank,' 'Starbuck's Coffee', etc.).

To be sure, from a purely linguistic point of view this is not the soundest way of proceeding. However, in view of the fact that a very large amount of data had to be classified on the spot, a quick and easily applicable method was preferred over one that would have been more sophisticated but at the same time more complicated when put into oper-ation. Some of the problems to this approach will become evident in section 5.9.

The survey was conducted between February and May 2003, on working days between 11.00 a.m. and 5.00 p.m. Since shops often display parts of their commodities outside on the pavement, only days with stable weather conditions were selected for research. The data were collected by myself in 26 areas, and in one area each by Masato Yoneda (National Institute for Japanese Language) and Min-Ho Yang (Tohoku University). In order to guarantee methodological consistency, I reiter-ated the procedure at all 28 areas before starting to analyse the data. All multilingual signs were recorded by digital camera. With few exceptions (see 5.8 and 5.10), signs categorised as monolingual were not taken into further consideration.

Within the 28 survey areas a total of 11,834 signs were counted, of which 2444 were categorised as multilingual. They constitute the sample of this study. The ratio of multilingual signs is 20.7% in total and 24.1%

**Table 5.2** Survey areas and signs

| No. | Area name | Area code | Items counted | Monol. signs | Multil. signs | Multil. signs (%) | Distance (m) |
|---|---|---|---|---|---|---|---|
| 1 | Tōkyō | tok | 87 | 45 | 42 | 48.3 | 90 |
| 2 | Kanda | kan | 490 | 400 | 90 | 18.4 | 122 |
| 3 | Akihabara | aki | 1054 | 910 | 144 | 13.7 | 190 |
| 4 | Okachimachi | oka | 550 | 490 | 60 | 10.9 | 65 |
| 5 | Ueno | uen | 103 | 75 | 28 | 27.2 | 263 |
| 6 | Uguisudani | ugu | 224 | 140 | 84 | 37.5 | 240 |
| 7 | Nishinippori | nis | 544 | 480 | 64 | 11.8 | 160 |
| 8 | Tabata | tab | 495 | 430 | 65 | 13.1 | 170 |
| 9 | Komagome | kom | 630 | 480 | 150 | 23.8 | 210 |
| 10 | Sugamo | sug | 701 | 540 | 161 | 23.0 | 200 |
| 11 | Ōtsuka | ots | 301 | 250 | 51 | 16.9 | 90 |
| 12 | Ikebukuro | ike | 350 | 240 | 110 | 31.4 | 110 |
| 13 | Mejiro | mio | 138 | 90 | 48 | 34.8 | 255 |
| 14 | Takadanobaba | tak | 656 | 540 | 116 | 17.7 | 120 |
| 15 | Shin-Ōkubo | sok | 717 | 580 | 137 | 19.1 | 175 |
| 16 | Shinjuku | sju | 339 | 260 | 79 | 23.3 | 75 |
| 17 | Yoyogi | yoy | 141 | 110 | 31 | 22.0 | 90 |
| 18 | Harajuku | har | 272 | 160 | 112 | 41.2 | 130 |
| 19 | Shibuya | sbu | 682 | 510 | 172 | 25.2 | 160 |
| 20 | Ebisu | ebi | 309 | 250 | 59 | 19.1 | 80 |
| 21 | Meguro | meg | 714 | 640 | 74 | 10.4 | 120 |
| 22 | Gotanda | got | 474 | 410 | 64 | 13.5 | 80 |
| 23 | Ōsaki | osa | 292 | 180 | 112 | 38.4 | 150 |
| 24 | Shinagawa | sna | 234 | 150 | 84 | 35.9 | 400 |
| 25 | Tamachi | tam | 376 | 300 | 76 | 20.2 | 270 |
| 26 | Hamamatsuchō | ham | 380 | 290 | 90 | 23.7 | 105 |
| 27 | Shinbashi | sin | 406 | 330 | 76 | 18.7 | 90 |
| 28 | Yūrakuchō | yur | 175 | 110 | 65 | 37.1 | 95 |
| | **Sum** | | **11,834** | **9390** | **2444** | | |

average per survey area. The relative frequency of multilingual signs varies highly with regard to location, ranging from over 48% in the survey area around Tōkyō Station, to little more than 10% in the survey area in Meguro. The standard deviation is 10.2.

Starting from Tōkyō in the east of the Yamanote Line loop, the survey areas are arrayed counter-clockwise in consecutive order in Table 5.2 (see also Figure 5.1 on p. 89). The area codes given in the table are part of the specific survey number assigned to each sign of the sample. For instance, the 42 multilingual signs in the area around Tōkyō Station have been numbered in order of appearance from 'tok001' to 'tok042'. Note that the alternative spelling 'Tōkyō' is used to distinguish the survey area from the city as a whole, which I will continue to refer to as 'Tokyo'. If signs not part of the sample are discussed, they are indicated by a '+' between area code and two-digit number.

A closer analysis of the data will be given in subsequent sections. We will start with some general observations about the two most basic variables: the languages contained and their combinations.

## 5.2 Languages Contained

The languages contained on a multilingual sign were determined by the same rules that had been applied to distinguish between monolingual and multilingual signs (see 5.1). Anything written in Kanji, Kana, or Kanji and Kana was counted as Japanese, irrespective of whether or not borrowings or ad hoc transliterations of vocabulary from other languages were contained. This category will be referred to as 'Japanese in Kanji & Kana'. Three other options for writing Japanese were assigned to a different category each: Japanese in Roman alphabet, Japanese in Braille, and Japanese with Kanji annotated by Furigana (see 3.10). Unless explicitly mentioned, the term 'Japanese' henceforth means Japanese in Kanji & Kana. The three other script options will be referred to as 'Japanese glosses'.

A coherent phrase was never counted as both English and Romanised Japanese but assigned to one of the two. Only phrases not containing English elements were counted as Romanised Japanese. All other cases were counted as English. This includes topographic information combining transliterated and translated elements, for instance 'Kyufurukawa Garden' (kom005), or frequently found cases of double representations (see 5.9), such as 'Mejiro dōri Ave.' [lit. Mejiro Street Avenue; mio025]. Likewise, transliterated Japanese terms combined with English elements, for instance 'NEW EBI BURGER' (ike086) or 'FASHION SHOES IZUMI' (oka029), were counted as English and not as Romanised Japanese.

All languages other than Japanese were identified only when represented in their customary scripts: Chinese in long- or short-style characters; Korean in Hangul; English, French, etc. in the Roman alphabet; Arabic and Persian in the Arabic script; Thai in the Thai script; etc. Japanese Kanji characters often coincide with characters used for writing Chinese, but, unless there was a clear indication that they represented Chinese, they were counted as Japanese (see 5.3 and 5.9). Doubtful items in Western languages were categorised as English. A sign with the single term 'Information' (aki093), for instance, was not counted as, say, French or German.

Apart from Japanese in the four graphic representations mentioned above, 14 other languages were identified on the 2444 signs of the sample. They are listed in Table 5.3. English has the highest frequency of occurrence by a large measure. It is contained on almost 93% of all signs of the sample. This predominance is so salient that one may say that

**Table 5.3** Languages and Japanese glosses on the signs of the sample

| Languages/J. glosses | Contained | % of cases |
|---|---|---|
| Japanese | | |
| in Kanji & Kana | 1779 | 72.8 |
| in Roman alphabet | 224 | 9.2 |
| with Furigana | 73 | 3.0 |
| in Braille | 20 | 0.8 |
| English | 2266 | 92.7 |
| Chinese | 62 | 2.5 |
| Korean | 40 | 1.6 |
| French | 20 | 0.8 |
| Portuguese | 12 | 0.5 |
| Spanish | 8 | 0.3 |
| Latin | 6 | 0.3 |
| Thai | 5 | 0.2 |
| Italian | 4 | 0.2 |
| Persian | 2 | 0.1 |
| Tagalog | 2 | 0.1 |
| German | 2 | 0.1 |
| Arabic | 1 | 0.0 |
| Russian | 1 | 0.0 |
| **Total cases** | **2444** | **100** |

multilingualism in Tokyo's linguistic landscape is for the most part Japanese–English bilingualism. The strength of English becomes clear when compared to all languages other than Japanese, which, though recognisable, quantitatively make up a minor part of the sample only. There are only two other foreign languages with a ratio higher than 1%: Chinese (2.5%) and Korean (1.6%). Most other languages appear on fewer than 10 signs of the sample.

Around 73% of the survey items contain Japanese in Kanji & Kana. This is noticeably less than the ratio of English. In other words, multilingual signs not containing Japanese in Kanji & Kana are more frequent than multilingual signs not containing English. While English is not available on only 178 signs of the sample, 665 survey items do not contain Japanese in Kanji & Kana. However, in view of the fact that some 9390 Japanese-only signs found in the survey areas have been excluded from the sample, this outcome is difficult to interpret.

A noteworthy point is the relatively high frequency of Romanised Japanese. Though text in the Roman alphabet was only counted as Japanese when appearing in English-free environments, the ratio for Romanised Japanese is just below 10%. This suggests that Roman letters are an option more frequently used for writing Japanese than one might commonly expect (see also Stanlaw, 2004: 152–6). Being contained on around 3% of the signs of the sample, Japanese with Furigana still scores higher than Chinese and Korean. Braille was found on 0.8% of the signs, a frequency in the same range as that of French.

I have already pointed out that the various options of graphically representing Japanese constitute an important part of the city's multilingualism. However, it is worth taking a look at the situation if only the first part of the underlying definition of a multilingual sign – a sign containing at least one language in addition to, or instead of, Japanese (see 5.1) – was considered relevant. A model calculation of the results, based on the data of the present survey, is given in Table 5.4. If Furigana supplementations and Japanese in the Roman alphabet or in Braille are not included in the definition, some items fall out of the sample. The number of multilingual signs decreases from 2444 to 2321, which would be a ratio of 19.6% multilingual signs. Consequently, languages other than Japanese slightly rise in frequency, with English coming very close to 100%. Only 55 items not containing English would be left. All in all, however, a comparison of Tables 5.3 and 5.4 reveals that there are no major contortions if both parts of the suggested definition are applied. Neither the overall frequency of multilingual signs nor the breakdown of the languages contained exhibit larger deviations. Subsequent analysis will therefore work within the broader frame, including different graphic representations of Japanese.

**Table 5.4** Languages on the signs of the sample

| Language | Contained | % of cases |
|---|---|---|
| Japanese | 1674 | 72.1 |
| English | 2266 | 97.6 |
| Chinese | 62 | 2.7 |
| Korean | 40 | 1.7 |
| French | 20 | 0.9 |
| Portuguese | 12 | 0.5 |
| Spanish | 8 | 0.3 |
| Latin | 6 | 0.3 |
| Thai | 5 | 0.2 |
| Italian | 4 | 0.2 |
| Persian | 2 | 0.1 |
| Tagalog | 2 | 0.1 |
| German | 2 | 0.1 |
| Arabic | 1 | 0.0 |
| Russian | 1 | 0.0 |
| **Total cases** | **2321** | **100** |

## 5.3 Combinations

This section takes a closer look at the combination patterns of languages and Japanese glosses on the signs of the sample. For a general overview the data have been organised in Table 5.5 according to the model used by Inoue (2000; see 3.10). The 14 foreign languages and four possible graphic representations of Japanese multiply into 36 combinations. They have been arranged in order of frequency. The two combinations most strongly represented are Japanese–English, with 57.3% (No. 1), and English-only, with 25.2% (No. 2). They make up over 80% of the sample. Only four other combinations occur more than once in a hundred signs (Nos. 3, 4, 5, and 6): Japanese in Kanji & Kana and Japanese in the Roman alphabet (4.2%); Japanese in Kanji & Kana, Japanese in the Roman alphabet, and English (3.9%); Japanese, English, and Chinese (1.7%); and Japanese in Kanji & Kana, with Furigana supplementations, and English (1.4%).

A look at the bottom line of Table 5.5 shows that languages with a low total frequency occur in few combinations. Russian, Arabic, German, Tagalog, and Persian are part of only one pattern, Latin and Thai of two. Because most of these languages are contained on only one sign or on

**Table 5.5** Combination patterns

| No. | J-k | J-r | J-f | J-b | E | C | K | F | PO | S | L | TH | I | PE | TA | G | A | R | Sum | % of cases |
|---|---|---|---|---|---|---|---|---|---|---|---|---|---|---|---|---|---|---|---|---|
| 1 | 1 | | | | 1 | | | | | | | | | | | | | | 2 | 57.3 |
| 2 | 1 | | | | 1 | | | | | | | | | | | | | | 1 | 25.2 |
| 3 | 1 | 1 | | | | | | | | | | | | | | | | | 2 | 4.2 |
| 4 | 1 | 1 | | | 1 | 1 | | | | | | | | | | | | | 3 | 3.9 |
| 5 | 1 | | | | 1 | | | | | | | | | | | | | | 3 | 1.7 |
| 6 | 1 | | 1 | | 1 | | | | | | | | | | | | | | 3 | 1.4 |
| 7 | 1 | | 1 | | 1 | | | | | | | | | | | | | | 2 | 0.8 |
| 8 | 1 | | | | | | 1 | | | | | | | | | | | | 2 | 0.5 |
| 9 | | 1 | | | 1 | | | | | | | | | | | | | | 2 | 0.4 |
| 10 | 1 | | | 1 | | | | | | | | | | | | | | | 2 | 0.4 |
| 11 | 1 | | 1 | 1 | 1 | | 1 | | | | | | | | | | | | 4 | 0.4 |
| 12 | 1 | | 1 | | 1 | | | | | | | | | | | | | | 2 | 0.3 |
| 13 | 1 | 1 | 1 | | 1 | | 1 | | | | | | | | | | | | 4 | 0.3 |
| 14 | | | | | | | | | 1 | | | | | | | | | | 1 | 0.3 |
| 15 | | | | | 1 | 1 | | | | | | | | | | | | | 3 | 0.2 |
| 16 | 1 | | | | | 1 | | | | | | | | | | | | | 2 | 0.2 |
| 17 | 1 | | | | 1 | | 1 | | | | | | | | | | | | 3 | 0.2 |
| 18 | 1 | | | | | | | 1 | | | | | | | | | | | 2 | 0.2 |
| 19 | 1 | | | | | | | | | | 1 | | | | | | | | 2 | 0.2 |
| 20 | | 1 | | | | | | 1 | | | | | | | | | | | 2 | 0.2 |

**Table 5.5** continued

| No. | J-k | J-r | J-f | J-b | E | C | K | F | PO | S | L | TH | I | PE | TA | G | A | R | Sum | % of cases |
|---|---|---|---|---|---|---|---|---|---|---|---|---|---|---|---|---|---|---|---|---|
| 21 | | | | | | | | 1 | | | | | | | | | | | 1 | 0.2 |
| 22 | 1 | | | | 1 | 1 | 1 | | | | | | | | | | | | 4 | 0.2 |
| 23 | 1 | | | | 1 | | | 1 | | | | | | | | | | | 3 | 0.2 |
| 24 | 1 | | | | 1 | | | | | 1 | | | | | | | | | 3 | 0.2 |
| 25 | 1 | | | | | | | | | | | 1 | | | | | | | 2 | 0.1 |
| 26 | | | | | | | | | 1 | | | | | | | | | | 1 | 0.1 |
| 27 | | 1 | | | 1 | | | 1 | | 1 | | | 1 | | | 1 | | | 6 | 0.1 |
| 28 | 1 | | | | 1 | 1 | 1 | | 1 | 1 | | 1 | | 1 | 1 | | | | 9 | 0.1 |
| 29 | 1 | | | | | 1 | 1 | | | | | | | | | | | | 3 | 0.0 |
| 30 | 1 | | | | 1 | 1 | | | | | | | | | | | 1 | | 4 | 0.0 |
| 31 | 1 | | | | 1 | | | | | | | | 1 | | | | | | 3 | 0.0 |
| 32 | 1 | 1 | | | 1 | | | | | | 1 | | | | | | | | 4 | 0.0 |
| 33 | 1 | | | | | | | | | | | | 1 | | | | | | 2 | 0.0 |
| 34 | 1 | | | | | | | | 1 | | | | | | | | | | 2 | 0.0 |
| 35 | | 1 | | | | | | | | | | | | | | | | | 1 | 0.0 |
| 36 | | | | | | | | | | | | | | | | | | 1 | 1 | 0.0 |
| **Sum** | 25 | 8 | 4 | 2 | 19 | 7 | 7 | 5 | 4 | 3 | 2 | 2 | 3 | 1 | 1 | 1 | 1 | 1 | | 100 |

*Notes:* J-k=Japanese in Kanji & Kana, J-r=Romanised Japanese, J-f=Furigana supplementations, J-b=Japanese in Braille, E=English, C=Chinese, K=Korean, F=French, PO=Portuguese, S=Spanish, L=Latin, TH=Thai, I=Italian, PE=Persian, TA=Tagalog, G=German, A=Arabic, R=Russian.

several signs with identical design, this does not call for any further interpretation. As to the most frequent combination patterns, there are some interesting differences to the overall frequency of occurrence discussed in the previous section. Table 5.6 shows that the languages and Japanese glosses that appear in the highest number of combinations are not identical to those most frequently found on the signs in total. Japanese in Kanji & Kana is part of 25 combinations, six more than English, although, as we have seen, English is contained on far more signs of the sample than Japanese. Also, Japanese with Furigana ranks higher in overall frequency than in combination patterns. This can be ascribed to the fact that Furigana has to co-appear with Kanji otherwise it would not be recognisable as Furigana (see 3.10). Deviations in ranking between combination patterns and general frequency are therefore diffi-cult to evaluate. In general, however, Japanese seems to combine more easily than English.

Not only Furigana but also Braille appears only in combination with Japanese in Kanji & Kana (Nos. 10 and 11 in Table 5.5), whereas Japanese in the Roman alphabet occurs on signs without the latter, too (Nos. 9, 20, 27, and 36). There are only 18 such signs in total but they deserve special attention. Provided that a corresponding version of the sign in Kanji & Kana was not available on another sign in close proximity (see 5.8), the choice of the script on these signs implies that not only foreigners but also Japanese are expected to read the Romanised version. While most of these signs provide transliterations of Japanese place or person names, the Roman alphabet in some cases is also employed for common nouns or even whole sentences in Japanese. One such example is a slogan by a major Japanese telephone company that was found several times within the 28 survey areas (aki118, sug129, sok124–125, sbu110–111). The text contained, meaning something like 'The slogan is also important, but most important is making it real', is as follows:

**Table 5.6** Ranking: frequency of occurrence vs. combinations

| Languages/J. glosses | Ranking: contained | Ranking: combinations |
| --- | --- | --- |
| English | 1 | 2 |
| Japanese (Kanji & Kana) | 2 | 1 |
| Japanese (Romanised) | 3 | 3 |
| Japanese (Furigana) | 4 | 7 |
| Chinese | 5 | 4 |
| Korean | 6 | 4 |
| French | 7 | 6 |

SUROUGAN MO
DAIJIDAKEREDO,
JIKKOUSURUNOGA,
ICHIBAN DAIJI.

Another point that lends itself to quantitative analysis is the number of languages or Japanese glosses combined on the 2444 signs of the sample. The range goes from one to nine, but it is self-evident from the frequency values in Table 5.5 that an overwhelming majority of the signs contain either two (64.6%) or only one language or Japanese gloss (25.9%). The average number per sign is 1.85. The data are given in Table 5.7.

The two items with nine languages are the front and backside of a sign at a small international telephone company in Ōsaki (osa059–060). The slogan 'Calling from Japan' is given in Japanese, English, Chinese, Korean, Spanish, Portuguese, Thai, Persian, and Tagalog. Two stickers found in the Shinjuku area (sju032–033) contain six languages. Their offer to buy tickets for the Soccer World Cup finals in 2002 is made in Romanised Japanese, English, French, Spanish, Italian, and German.

The next category is signs with four languages or Japanese glosses. The 24 items fall into three major groups: (1) 10 signs are explanation plates on postboxes in Japanese, with Furigana and in Braille, and in English (e.g. tok036–037); (2) eight signs contain Japanese in Kanji & Kana, with occasional Furigana, Japanese in the Roman alphabet, and English. Most of these signs are maps (e.g. ugu007) or parts of emergency signage (e.g. ugu030); and (3) four signs contain Japanese, English, Chinese, and Korean: a sign in front of the National Science Museum in Ueno (uen004), an explanation sign about garbage collection in Nishinippori (nis027), in addition to a prohibition on parking bicycles (sok030) and an evacuation area sign (sok040), both in Shin-Ōkubo. Though the overall number of signs with four languages or Japanese

**Table 5.7** Number of languages and Japanese glosses contained

| *Number of languages/J. glosses* | *Cases* | *%* |
|---|---|---|
| n = 9 | 2 | 0.1 |
| n = 6 | 2 | 0.1 |
| n = 4 | 24 | 1.0 |
| n = 3 | 203 | 8.3 |
| n = 2 | 1579 | 64.6 |
| n = 1 | 634 | 25.9 |
| **Total** | **2444** | **100** |

glosses is rather small, the three combination patterns are relatively fixed for this group of signs (see Table 5.8).

Signs containing one, two, or three languages or Japanese glosses are too large in number to be discussed one by one. However, some general tendencies can be observed here, too. Signs with three languages or Japanese glosses fall into three main groups, which account for more than 80% of the trilingual items: (1) signs with Japanese in Kanji & Kana, Japanese in the Roman alphabet, and English; (2) signs with Japanese, English, and Chinese; and (3) signs with Japanese, supplemented by Furigana, and English. The seven other combinations are of minor quantitative importance (see Table 5.9).

We have already seen that signs with two languages or Japanese glosses are the most frequent type of multilingual sign. Almost 90% of these are Japanese–English signs. Signs with Japanese in Kanji & Kana and Japanese in the Roman alphabet still have some quantitative significance, while the 11 other combinations of this category add up to less than 5% (see Table 5.10).

**Table 5.8** Combinations on signs with four languages or Japanese glosses

| Combinations | Cases |
|---|---|
| J-k, J-f, J-b, E | 10 |
| J-k, J-f, J-r, E | 8 |
| J-k, E, C, K | 4 |
| Others | 2 |
| **Sum** | **24** |

*Notes*: J-k=Japanese in Kanji & Kana, J-r=Romanised Japanese, J-f=Furigana supplementations, J-b=Japanese in Braille, E=English, C=Chinese, K=Korean.

**Table 5.9** Combinations on signs with three languages or Japanese glosses

| Combinations | Cases | % |
|---|---|---|
| J-k, J-r, E | 95 | 46.8 |
| J-k, E, C | 42 | 20.7 |
| J-k, J-f, E | 35 | 17.2 |
| Others | 31 | 15.3 |
| **Sum** | **203** | **100** |

*Notes*: J-k=Japanese in Kanji & Kana, J-r=Romanised Japanese, J-f=Furigana supplementations, E=English, C=Chinese.

Signs with only one language are by and large signs in English. As can be seen in Table 5.11, over 97% of all items in this category are English-only signs. Other 'autonomous' languages (Bagna & Barni, 2006; see 3.8) are Korean, French, Portuguese, Russian, and Romanised Japanese. They will be briefly discussed in turn.

Korean is the only language on eight signs, all of which were found within the Shin-Okubo area (sok019, sok031, sok035, sok039, sok083–085). This accumulation will be given closer attention when examining the geographic distribution of multilingual signs in section 5.5. Three of the French-only signs are shop signs of a 'Salon de Thé Colombin' in Harajuku (har086–088), and a fourth one was found outside an apartment building in Uguisudani named 'HABITATION FORÊT' (ugu032). The Portuguese-only signs were situated in the area in Gotanda. Two were set up at a photo studio (got004–005), and a third one was attached to the door of a telephone shop (got009). The photo studio displayed some more Portuguese signs, which were not included in the sample because they had been put up slightly outside the delineated limits of

**Table 5.10** Combinations on signs with two languages or Japanese glosses

| *Combinations* | *Cases* | % |
|---|---|---|
| J-k, E | 1401 | 88.7 |
| J-k, J-r | 102 | 6.5 |
| Others | 76 | 4.8 |
| **Sum** | **1579** | **100** |

*Notes*: J-k=Japanese in Kanji & Kana, J-r=Romanised Japanese, E=English.

**Table 5.11** Signs with only one language

| *Language* | *Cases* |
|---|---|
| English | 617 |
| Korean | 8 |
| French | 4 |
| Portuguese | 3 |
| Russian | 1 |
| Rom. Japanese | 1 |
| **Sum** | **634** |

the survey area. The proximity of the Brazilian consulate, situated at an adjacent street block, is most likely to account for this concentration of Portuguese-only signs.

The telephone shop in Gotanda also provided the one Russian-only sign (got008). It contained the same message as the sign in Portuguese (got009) and a third one in English (got007; see Figure 5.17 on p. 113). All three signs were attached in close proximity to each other. They were counted as three separate one-language items rather than one trilingual sign because, as described in section 5.1, the determination of survey items is based on spatial rather than semantic categories. The only sign containing Romanised Japanese was found in the Tōkyō area, where it displayed the address of the place, 'Chiyoda-ku Marunouchi 1–2' (tok027). Some metres further on, a sign in identical design with the same message in Japanese in Kanji & Kana was put up. These examples show that the occurrence of a sign with one language or Japanese gloss does not necessarily mean that there was no translation or transliteration available. This problem will be discussed in more detail in section 5.8.

The sample does not contain any Chinese-only signs, though Chinese ranks higher in total frequency of appearance than Korean, French, and Russian. This is partially due to the fact that a few apparent Chinese-only candidates contained a certain number of letters that could not be assigned to either of the sets of Chinese long- or short-style characters, respectively. They were only recognisable as Japanese Kanji. We will come back to these instances of script-mixing in section 5.9. Another reason for the absence of Chinese-only signs will become apparent in the next section, which takes a closer look at the originators of multilingual signs.

## 5.4 Top-down vs. Bottom-up

One of the key variables with regard to the question *Linguistic landscaping by whom?* is the distinction between official and non-official signs. Landry and Bourhis, in their seminal paper, make the following distinction between private signs and government signs:

> Private signs include commercial signs on storefronts and business institutions (e.g., retail stores and banks), commercial advertising on billboards, and advertising signs displayed in public transport and on private vehicles. Government signs refer to public signs used by national, regional, or municipal governments in the following domains: road signs, place names, street names, and inscriptions on government buildings including ministries, hospitals, universities, town halls, schools, metro stations, and public parks. (1997: 26–7)

Similar distinctions have been made in other previous studies: Scollon and Scollon (2003; see 3.7) differentiate between municipal and commercial discourses; Calvet (1990, 1994; see 3.5) juxtaposes 'in vitro' and 'in vivo' policies; and Ben-Rafael *et al.* (2004, 2006; see 3.3) identify top-down and bottom-up forces in linguistic landscaping. Taking up this latter terminology, all government-related signs of the Tokyo sample have been classified as top-down signs. These are mainly signs by the ward administrations, the Tokyo Metropolitan Government, or an agency of the national government. In addition, all signs related to public transport facilities and Japan Post have been counted as top-down signs. All other signs have been considered bottom-up signs. Except for a few special cases the classification of the two did not prove too difficult. In alternation with the terms 'top-down' and 'bottom-up' the expressions 'official' and 'non-official' will be used to distinguish the two categories throughout this chapter.

Table 5.12 gives the proportion of the two types of signs for the 2444 survey items. With around 30%, top-down signs make up the numerical minority. This shows that the multilingual landscape in Tokyo is shaped more by the citizens than by the authorities. On the other hand, it is undeniable that official agencies have their share in this process, too. This is a major difference to the situation in Dakar, where Calvet (1990, 1994; see 3.5) has criticised that, despite the multilingual make-up of the population, top-down signs were available only in the official language, French. In Tokyo we find a somewhat reversed picture. Though the population of the city is predominantly Japanese, official language policies have been designed to include languages other than Japanese on public signs. Since the early 1990s various administrative guidelines have been issued to this effect (e.g. Shinagawa Ward, 1994; TMG, 1991, 1997, 2003; see Backhaus, 2004: 46–51). While these guidelines used to focus exclusively on English, the most recent of them, the Tokyo Metropolitan Government's *Guide for Making City Writing Easy to Understand Also to Foreigners* (TMG, 2003: 9), contains the following directions:

**Table 5.12** Top-down (official) vs. bottom-up (non-official) signs

| *Type of sign* | *Cases* | *%* |
|---|---|---|
| Top-down | 701 | 28.7 |
| Bottom-up | 1743 | 71.3 |
| **Total** | **2444** | **100** |

(1) Rōmaji (English)
   In principle, all Japanese writing is given together with Rōmaji (English).
   . . .

(2) Rōmaji (English) + a number of other languages
   In view of the number of registered foreign residents and foreign travellers in Tokyo, four languages are used preferentially: Japanese, Rōmaji (English), Chinese (short-type characters), and Hangul [*sic*].
   . . .

(3) Furigana
   Mainly thinking of foreigners who are living in Tokyo as target group, annotating Kanji with Furigana will have some effect, too.

In order to examine how far these guidelines have been applied in practice, we will now take a closer look at which languages and Japanese glosses appear on which of the two types of signs. Table 5.13 gives a cross-tabulation of the two variables. It shows that 10 languages appear only on bottom-up signs: French, Portuguese, Spanish, Thai, Italian, Persian, Tagalog, German, Arabic, and Russian. Languages eligible to be contained on top-down signs are Japanese (in all four graphic representations), English, Chinese, Korean, and Latin. Three botanic explanation plates with Latin nomenclature excluded, one can recognise the four languages mentioned in the above-cited guidelines. These findings suggest that, if a language other than the four is contained on a sign in central Tokyo, it will not be an official sign.

Whereas English tends to appear more frequently on bottom-up signs, Japanese is predominantly found on top-down signs. In total, over 97% of all top-down signs contain Japanese. Hence there are almost no official signs not containing the national language, while more than one-third of all non-official multilingual signs obviously can do without. Similar differences to those between Japanese and English apply to Chinese and Korean. While the majority of Chinese signs are set up by official agencies, most items containing Korean are bottom-up signs. Unless private agents, presumably Tokyo's Korean population, put up signs in their language by themselves, Korean would be virtually absent from the city's linguistic landscape. The fact that it is displayed on just five official signs in total suggests an apparent gap between theory and practice in official sign writing. It must be kept in mind, however, that the 2003 guidelines by the time of the survey had only just been issued.

A noteworthy point about Japanese glosses is that signs containing Japanese in Braille are exclusively top-down signs. The signs in question

**Table 5.13** Top-down/bottom-up signs vs. languages/Japanese glosses
contained

| Languages/J. glosses | Top-down signs (n = 701) | Bottom-up signs (n = 1743) |
|---|---|---|
| Japanese | | |
|    in Kanji & Kana | 97.6% | 62.8% |
|    in Roman alphabet | 20.8% | 4.5% |
|    with Furigana | 9.1% | 0.5% |
|    in Braille | 2.9% | – |
| English | 83.7% | 96.3% |
| Chinese | 6.4% | 1.0% |
| Korean | 0.7% | 2.0% |
| French | – | 1.1% |
| Portuguese | – | 0.7% |
| Spanish | – | 0.5% |
| Latin | 0.4% | 0.2% |
| Thai | – | 0.3% |
| Italian | – | 0.2% |
| Persian | – | 0.1% |
| Tagalog | – | 0.1% |
| German | – | 0.1% |
| Arabic | – | 0.1% |
| Russian | – | 0.1% |

are information plates on postboxes, which will be discussed in more
detail in sections 5.9 and 5.10. The distribution of Furigana supplementations shows a similar tendency, with only nine of the 73 signs classified
as bottom-up. The presence of Braille, Furigana, and Chinese in public
space is thus mainly the result of official language policies.

In general, the distinction between top-down and bottom-up signs
shows that both official and non-official agents are involved in shaping
Tokyo's multilingual landscape. However, the two types of sign writers
have markedly different preferences in their choice of languages.
Messages of official origin are available in Japanese, English, Chinese,
and, to some extent, Korean and Latin. All other languages have to be
provided by non-official sign writers. Some more qualitative differences
between the two types of signs will come to light in subsequent sections.

## 5.5 Geographic Distribution

Geographic distribution is another relevant variable with regard to the making of the linguistic landscape. Many previous studies have observed characteristic patterns concerning the visibility of a language in given parts of the place under observation. Two examples where this has been particularly salient are Brussels and Montreal (see 3.1 and 3.2). In both cities we have two major linguistic groups whose geographic distribution over the territory has been found reflected in the relative availability or non-availability of their languages on signs. This section examines whether there are any comparable patterns in the geographic distribution of languages on signs in Tokyo.

According to statistics by the Tokyo Metropolitan Government, the total population of the 23 wards, which constitute the central parts of Tokyo, by the time of the survey in 2003 was 8,129,801 people. A little fewer than 300,000 of these were non-Japanese nationals, a ratio of 3.6%. Note that a considerable number of non-registered foreigners as well as naturalised Japanese citizens are not included in this figure. Over 80% of the 23 wards' registered foreign residents are from Asian countries, mainly from China (35%) and the Korean peninsula (29%). People from Europe (7%) and North America (6%) make up two smaller recognisable groups, while foreign residents from other parts of the world are rather weakly represented (TMG, 2004c, 2004d).

Table 5.14 gives an overview of the numbers of foreign residents and their countries of origin for each of the 23 wards. With over 10%, Shinjuku (10.8%) and Minato (10.3%) have the highest share of non-Japanese population. They are followed by Arakawa (7.4%), Toshima (7.1%), Taitō (6.3%), and Shibuya (5.9%). Setagaya (1.9%) and Nerima (1.9%) at the lower end of the scale still have a higher proportion of registered foreigners than the national average of 1.5%. As to the spatial distribution of foreigners in Tokyo, three main tendencies are commonly referred to (e.g. Tanaka, 2000: 18; Yonehara, 1997: 140): (1) People from Asia are concentrated in the wards situated in the north and north-west of central Tokyo. An overall trend here is that (2) long-term foreign residents are frequently found in the northern wards, particularly Kita, Adachi, Arakawa, and Taitō, whereas people who have relatively recently come to Japan tend to live closer to the centre, in Shinjuku and Toshima Ward. (3) People from Western countries preferably settle in central or central-western wards such as Minato, Chiyoda, Shibuya, and Meguro.

Though Tokyo has not yet seen the formation of ethnic neighbourhoods comparable in scale to other major cities around the world, such developments have recently been discussed (Lützeler, 2002; Machimura, 2000; Okuda, 1994; Tajima, 1994). For instance, Kim (2003: 175) has observed that certain areas in Shinjuku Ward are increasingly acquiring

**Table 5.14** Foreign residents in Tokyo's 23 wards, as of 2003

| Ward | Countries of origin | | | Total |
|---|---|---|---|---|
| | *Asia* | *Europe & N. America* | *Others* | |
| Shinjuku | 9.4% | 1.1% | 0.3% | 10.8% |
| Minato | 4.4% | 4.9% | 1.0% | 10.3% |
| Arakawa | 7.1% | 0.2% | 0.1% | 7.4% |
| Toshima | 6.4% | 0.5% | 0.2% | 7.1% |
| Taitō | 5.9% | 0.3% | 0.1% | 6.3% |
| Shibuya | 2.7% | 2.7% | 0.5% | 5.9% |
| Chiyoda | 2.7% | 1.5% | 0.2% | 4.4% |
| Kita | 4.1% | 0.2% | 0.1% | 4.4% |
| Nakano | 3.2% | 0.4% | 0.3% | 3.9% |
| Bunkyō | 3.1% | 0.5% | 0.1% | 3.7% |
| Sumida | 3.3% | 0.2% | 0.1% | 3.6% |
| Kōtō | 3.2% | 0.2% | 0.1% | 3.5% |
| Adachi | 3.2% | 0.1% | 0.1% | 3.4% |
| Meguro | 2.1% | 1.0% | 0.2% | 3.3% |
| Edogawa | 2.9% | 0.1% | 0.1% | 3.1% |
| Shinagawa | 2.4% | 0.5% | 0.2% | 3.1% |
| Chūō | 2.3% | 0.6% | 0.1% | 3.0% |
| Itabashi | 2.8% | 0.2% | 0.0% | 3.0% |
| Katsushika | 2.5% | 0.1% | 0.1% | 2.7% |
| Ōta | 2.1% | 0.2% | 0.2% | 2.5% |
| Suginami | 1.8% | 0.3% | 0.1% | 2.2% |
| Setagaya | 1.2% | 0.5% | 0.2% | 1.9% |
| Nerima | 1.6% | 0.2% | 0.1% | 1.9% |

*Source*: TMG (2004c, 2004d)

traits of an ethnic Korean town. Waley gives the following account of the situation:

> Many of the large entertainment districts surrounding main-line railway stations in Tokyo (as in Osaka and other large cities) have links with Korean and Chinese (or Chinese–Taiwanese) capital dating back to the immediate post-war period. Some of these districts, notably parts of Ueno, Ikebukuro, and Shinjuku, have become increasingly distinct as 'ethnic' areas, with, for example, neon signs in Korean advertising restaurants. (2000: 152)

To what extent do our data corroborate these observations? The spatial distribution of foreign languages for the 28 areas is given in Table 5.15. It can be seen that eight areas do not contain any signs with foreign languages other than English: Tōkyō, Kanda, Akihabara, Okachimachi,

**Table 5.15** Spatial distribution of languages other than Japanese

| Survey area | Ward | E | C | K | F | PO | S | L | TH | I | PE | TA | G | A | R |
|---|---|---|---|---|---|---|---|---|---|---|---|---|---|---|---|
| Tōkyō | Chiyoda | 39 | | | | | | | | | | | | | |
| Kanda | Chiyoda | 85 | | | | | | | | | | | | | |
| Akihabara | Chiyoda | 137 | | | | | | | | | | | | | |
| Okachimachi | Taitō | 57 | | | | | | | | | | | | | |
| Ueno | Taitō | 27 | 1 | 1 | | | | | | | | | | | |
| Uguisudani | Taitō | 68 | | | 6 | | | | | | | | | | |
| Nishinippori | Arakawa | 55 | 1 | 1 | 5 | | | | | | | | | | |
| Tabata | Kita | 62 | | 1 | | | | | | | | | | | |
| Komagome | Bunkyō/Toshima | 145 | 1 | | | | | | | | | | | | |
| Sugamo | Toshima | 156 | 17 | | 1 | | | | | | | | | | |
| Ōtsuka | Toshima | | | 47 | | | | | | | | | | | |
| Ikebukuro | Toshima | 103 | 3 | | 3 | 1 | | | | 1 | | | | | |
| Mejiro | Toshima | 42 | 20 | | | | | 1 | | | | | | | |
| Takadanobaba | Shinjuku | 112 | 4 | | | | | | | | | | | | |
| Shin-Ōkubo | Shinjuku | 112 | 3 | 34 | | | | | | 1 | 1 | | | | |
| Shinjuku | Shinjuku | 79 | | | 2 | | 2 | | | 2 | | | 2 | | |
| Yoyogi | Shibuya | 28 | | | | | | | | | | | | | |
| Harajuku | Shibuya | 103 | 1 | | 3 | | | | 1 | | | | | | |
| Shibuya | Shibuya | 163 | 6 | | | 6 | 1 | | | | | | | | |
| Ebisu | Shibuya | 57 | | | | | 3 | | | | | | | | |
| Meguro | Shinagawa | 70 | | | | | | | | 2 | | | | | |
| Gotanda | Shinagawa | 58 | 1 | | 3 | | | | | | | | | | 1 |
| Ōsaki | Shinagawa | 107 | 2 | 2 | | 2 | 2 | 3 | 2 | | 2 | 2 | | | |
| Shinagawa | Minato | 75 | | | | | 1 | | | | | | | | |
| Tamachi | Minato | 72 | | | | | | | | | | | | | |
| Hamamatsuchō | Minato | 84 | 1 | | | | | | | | | | | | |
| Shinbashi | Minato | 70 | 2 | | | | | | | | | | | 1 | |
| Yūrakuchō | Chiyoda | 53 | | | | | | | | | | | | | |

*Notes*: E=English, C=Chinese, K=Korean, F=French, PO=Portuguese, S=Spanish, L=Latin, TH=Thai, I=Italian, PE=Persian, TA=Tagalog, G=German, A=Arabic, R=Russian.

Ōtsuka, Yoyogi, Tamachi, and Yūrakuchō. Conspicuous is a concentra-tion of five consecutive English-only areas in the east of the Yamanote loop. As illustrated in Figure 5.1 (p. 89), it stretches from Yūrakuchō to Okachimachi, including all four areas situated in Chiyoda Ward.

As to foreign languages other than English, it is problematic to look out for any geographic concentrations if the overall frequency of a certain lan-guage is only very low. If we determine 10% of the total of multilingual signs found in an area to be a critical value, three areas remain to be con-sidered. These are Sugamo and Mejiro for Chinese, and Shin-Ōkubo for Korean. The situation in these areas is summarised in Table 5.16.

The three areas are situated in the west-north-western parts of the Yamanote loop, in Shinjuku (Shin-Ōkubo) and Toshima (Sugamo and Mejiro). As shown above, these are two wards where the share of foreign residents, especially from Asian countries, vis-à-vis the total ward popu-lation, is exceptionally large. That it is particularly people who have only recently come to Japan who settle in Shinjuku and Toshima suggests that these so-called 'newcomers' are having a stronger influence on the linguistic landscape than their compatriots who came decades earlier. The same tendency has been observed by Kim (2003, 2004) in a recent linguistic landscape study in Osaka.

A direct look at the Chinese and Korean signs in the three areas reveals some noteworthy qualitative differences between the two. All Chinese signs in Sugamo (sug105–121) and Mejiro (mio005–024) are of the same type – a Japanese–English–Chinese warning not to leave bicycles in the area. What we are actually dealing with is thus only one top-down sign appearing in frequent repetition. The originator of the sign is the Toshima ward administration. The English text of the sign, which was also found several times in the Ikebukuro area (ike025–028), is as follows (*sic*):

> This area is designated as a Bicycle & Motorbike NO Parking Area. Any bicycle left here will be impound in accordance with TOSIMA CITY Ordinance. To retrieve your bicycle,You must pay a removal fee of ¥3,000 (bicycle)or ¥5,000 (Motorbike).
> NOTE: Chains may be cut if necessary.

**Table 5.16** Areas with more than 10% multilingual signs in Chinese or Korean

| Survey area | Ward | Multil. signs | Signs cont. Chinese | Signs cont. Korean |
|---|---|---|---|---|
| Sugamo | Toshima | 161 | 10.6% | |
| Mejiro | Toshima | 48 | 41.7% | |
| Shin-Ōkubo | Shinjuku | 137 | 2.2% | 24.9% |

The situation of Korean signs in Shin-Ōkubo is much more variegated. Unlike in Sugamo and Mejiro, most of the signs in question are bottom-up signs. They have not been set up by official agents but by the keepers of the shops along the survey street, Ōkubo-dōri. Here we find signs of hairdressers (sok005) and beauty parlours (sok020), opticians (sok015), internet cafés (sok033), telephone shops (sok043), game centres (sok027), and various other smaller businesses. Only three of 34 signs containing Korean in Shin-Ōkubo are top-down signs, set up by the ward administration of Shinjuku: a small notice informing that a former garbage collection point is no longer serviced (sok025), a prohibition on parking bicycles (sok030), and an evacuation area map (sok040).

Korean in Shin-Ōkubo also differs from Chinese in Sugamo and Mejiro with regard to combination patterns and the question of 'autonomy' (Bagna & Barni, 2006; see 3.8). Whereas the Chinese texts on the parking prohibition for bicycles are accompanied by Japanese (and English), Korean in Shin-Ōkubo occasionally occurs in completely Japanese-free environments. As mentioned in section 5.3, there are no fewer than eight Korean-only signs within the 175 metres of the Shin-Ōkubo area. A further noteworthy pattern is the co-appearance of Korean and English on another seven signs that do not contain Japanese text (sok027–029, sok096–099). Though these signs are too small in number to permit any generalisations, the exclusion of Japanese is a highly noteworthy phenomenon. Borrowing from Calvet (1990: 175; see 3.5), we can interpret most of the Korean signs in Shin-Ōkubo as a means of taking possession – of 'marking the territory' by the Korean-speaking population. We may thus be witnessing first instances of how a non-Japanese population is about to take over parts of Tokyo's linguistic landscape. A telling example for this is a series of prefabricated Japanese signs papered over by handwritten Korean text to serve the shopkeeper's more immediate needs (sok083–085).

To summarise this section, the spatial distribution of languages other than Japanese on the signs of the sample in fact seems to reflect living patterns by Tokyo's foreign population. Two general tendencies can be made out: (1) a sequence of English-only areas in the eastern parts of the Yamanote Line loop, including one of the central wards in which Western foreigners are known to concentrate; and (2) larger occurrences of signs containing Chinese and Korean in the survey areas situated in the north-north-western parts of the loop. The basic picture is sketched in Figure 5.1.

The analysis of the data so far has been based completely on the mere appearance or non-appearance of a language or Japanese gloss on a sign, while no attention has been paid to functional aspects. These are the subject matter of the next section.

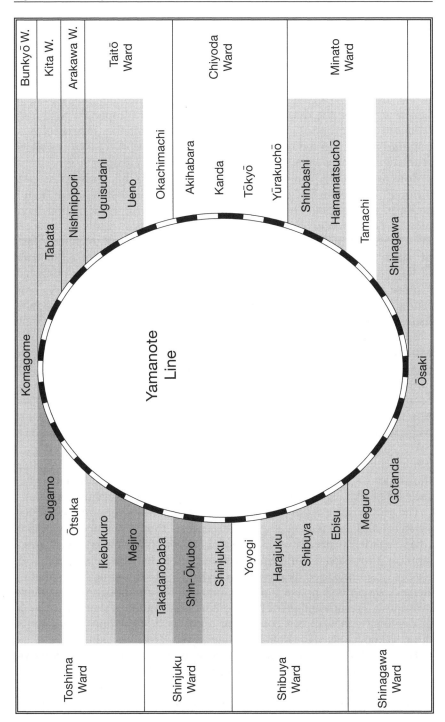

**Figure 5.1** Spatial distribution of languages other than Japanese

## 5.6 Part Writing

This section deals with the question of to what extent the texts contained on a sign constitute translations or transliterations of each other. Our aim is to get a better understanding of the problem of whether a given sign in the streets of Tokyo is multilingual (rather than monolingual Japanese, which would be the default case) more with regard to people with non-Japanese backgrounds or more with regard to the Japanese host population. As pointed out in Chapter 4, this is one of the key problems with regard to the question *Linguistic landscaping for whom?*

Borrowing terms from musicology, I will refer to this problem as 'part writing'. In the history of Western music a basic distinction is made between monophonic, homophonic, and polyphonic composition techniques. Monophony, the oldest of the three styles, refers to musical texture made up of a single unaccompanied melodic line called 'part' or 'voice'. A polyphonic composition combines a number of parts, each of which forms an individual melody. A homophonic composition has a more vertical structure. It features several parts that simultaneously follow the same melody. Usually, the highest of these tends to predominate, and there is little rhythmic differentiation across the lines.

Transferring these notions to language on signs, one can distinguish equivalent categories. Signs that display texts constituting a complete translation (or transliteration) of each other are homophonic signs. All of the texts contained convey the same content and in most cases it can be easily determined which of the texts is supposed to predominate (see 5.7). If only some content elements of a sign are available in two or more languages, the sign is still homophonic to some extent, but also has some parts scored for one language only. These are signs of a mixed part writing style. Signs with several languages that do not constitute mutual translations are polyphonic in style. They combine texts independent of each other. All signs with only one language are monophonic signs.

The part writing types defined here resemble the taxonomy developed by Reh (2004; see 3.6). A slight difference is that, for simplicity's sake, I have made no previous distinction between 'fragmentary' and 'overlapping' provision of multilingual information. For the time being, both types are summarised as mixed part writing. Monophonic signs, that is, signs containing only one foreign language, have not been part of Reh's taxonomy. The advantage of the present classification is that it is capable of dealing with samples containing signs with only one language. A direct comparison with Reh's terminology is given in Table 5.17.

The quantitative distribution of the signs of the sample is as follows. Mixed signs make up the largest group, with 841 items. Homophonic (638) and monophonic (614) signs are almost equal in frequency. The smallest group of signs are the 340 items identified as polyphonic signs

**Table 5.17** Four types of part writing, in comparison with Reh (2004)

| *Part writing types* | *Description* | *Types of multilingual writing defined by Reh (2004)* |
|---|---|---|
| Homophonic | Mutual translation or transliteration completely available | 'Duplicating' multilingualism |
| Mixed | Mutual translation or transliteration partially available | 'Fragmentary'/'overlapping' multilingualism |
| Polyphonic | Mutual translation or transliteration not available (two or more languages) | 'Complementary' multilingualism |
| Monophonic | Mutual translation or transliteration not available (one language) | |

**Table 5.18** Quantitative distribution of the four part writing types

| *Part writing type* | *Homophonic* | *Mixed* | *Polyphonic* | *Monophonic* | *Total\** |
|---|---|---|---|---|---|
| Cases | 638 | 841 | 340 | 614 | 2444 |
| % | 26.1 | 34.4 | 13.9 | 25.1 | 100 |

*\*Note*: Including 11 missing values.

(see Table 5.18). In order to illustrate the suggested classification, I will discuss some examples for each of the four part writing types in detail. Special attention will be given to the above-formulated question of why a sign has been produced in a multilingual rather than in a monolingual Japanese format.

## Homophonic signs

Homophonic signs contain two or more languages or Japanese glosses that constitute complete translations or transliterations of each other. This group of signs includes a few special cases where translations or transliterations were given on separate signs, identical in design and attached in close proximity (see 5.8). Two examples of homophonic signs are given in Figures 5.2 and 5.3: a fire hydrant indication (tab044) and a poster in the window of a telephone shop (tab006), both situated in the survey area in Tabata. The languages on the fire hydrant sign are English and Japanese; the text on the telephone poster is in Japanese,

**Figure 5.2** Fire hydrant sign (tab044)

**Figure 5.3** Poster at a telephone shop (tab006)

English, and Korean. Homophonic signs tend to contain relatively little text. There are only very few cases in which longer texts are completely available in more than one language. In this respect, the second example constitutes an exception. Despite the relatively large quantity of information, there is not a single detail that was not available in all three languages on the sign.

It is reasonable to assume that homophonic signs are multilingual as a result of considerations given to speakers of languages other than Japanese. As either size (tab044) or order (tab006) of the languages on the two example signs implies, the main language is Japanese (see also 5.7). Additional texts in other languages have been supplemented in order to make the message understandable also to people who do not know Japanese. The choice of a multilingual rather than a monolingual sign must have been made primarily with a foreign target group in mind.

## Mixed signs

Signs in a mixed style provide only some information in all languages or Japanese glosses. These types vary widely with regard to the amount of translated or transliterated contents. Two signs from the area in Komagome, given in Figures 5.4 and 5.5, will help to illustrate this point. One is a fire extinguisher box (kom042), the directions on which are almost completely available in both Japanese and English. The only piece of information offered in Japanese only is the instruction about where to point the hose after removing it. That it should best be directed towards the flames, however, is a rather self-evident if not dispensable detail. The sign thus comes very close to a homophonic sign and arguably might have been allocated to that category instead. The same cannot be said of the other example (kom001), a sign set up to inform passers-by about a nearby construction site. In this case only the most essential part of the message is available in English: 'UNDER CONSTRUCTION'. All further details concerning the object under construction, the organisations involved, the time it will take, etc. are confined to the Japanese version.

Most of the 841 items classified as mixed signs are somewhere between the two extremes. They provide the whole message in one language and varyingly large parts of it in one or several other languages or Japanese glosses. For the majority of cases the main version is in Japanese and the incomplete supplement is in English (or Romanised Japanese), just as in the two examples.

With regard to the type of Japanese-only information, a frequently found strategy for mixed signs is to omit details about place names. One characteristic type of sign applying this strategy is map boards. They

**Figure 5.4** Fire extinguisher (kom042)

**Figure 5.5** Construction site sign (kom001)

usually provide some of the Japanese place names in an additional translation or transliteration, while others remain without (tok016–017, aki107–110, ugu007–008, nis028–029, etc.). A similar example is street block signs giving only the name of the block but, unlike the corresponding Japanese version, not the name of the ward (tam001–004, ham020–021, etc.).

Another type of information easily omitted from translation is pragmatic details. Concerning the spatial deixis, for instance, the English versions on Japanese–English signs tend to lack information such as 'This is . . .' (nis001, meg011, etc.), '. . . inside this building' (ots023), or '. . . within five metres from here' (uen015). With regard to personal deixis one can observe how the expression of politeness in many cases remains confined to the Japanese version. Phrases such as *goenryo kudasai* [Please refrain from . . .] (osa006) or *gokyōryoku arigatō gozaimashita* [Thank you for your cooperation] (sbu063) are often available in Japanese but absent from the corresponding English text.

An illustrative example of this type of deictic omission is a sign at the entrance to an underground mall in Shinjuku (sju010). While the English version simply says 'NO SMOKING', the corresponding Japanese expressions *shūjitsu kin en* and *chikagai wa kin en desu* contain additional information about the temporal, spatial, and personal context of the discourse: that smoking is prohibited 'through the whole day' (*shūjitsu*), that this prohibition only applies to the inside of this mall (*chikagai*), and that this is a polite directive (the formal copula *desu*). None of this is contained in the English text.

Around two-thirds (68.9%) of the signs in mixed part writing style exhibit comparable patterns of information provision. For these signs a similar point as for homophonic signs can be made. The main motivation for preferring a multilingual design over one in Japanese only was to make an originally Japanese message available at least partially also to people not knowing Japanese. Such an interpretation seems much less feasible, however, to the residuary items in the group of mixed signs, to which we will turn now. A total of 151 signs give the complete information in a foreign language, mainly English, while the Japanese version covers only parts of it. Another 102 signs show what Reh (2004) has referred to as overlapping multilingualism. That is, the two or more versions each partially convey the same message and partially separate messages. The figures are summarised in Table 5.19.

Where more information is provided in the foreign language than in Japanese, various forms occur. One distinctive pattern is a duplicating information arrangement accompanied by a commercial name or catchphrase that is available only in the non-Japanese version. An example is Japanese–English stickers by various security companies (kan008,

**Table 5.19** Types of mixed signs

| Pattern | Case | % |
|---|---|---|
| Japanese version complete | 561 | 68.9 |
| Foreign version complete | 151 | 18.6 |
| Overlapping arrangement | 102 | 12.5 |
| **Sum** | **814** | **100** |

kan015, nis005, tab050, etc.). The warning that the place is being professionally monitored is proclaimed in either language, whereas the name of the company or a catch-phrase of it is available in English only.

Mixed signs with an overlapping information arrangement are very complex in nature. Since parts of the information are given only in one of the languages, in principle knowledge in all languages involved is a necessary requirement for a full understanding of the contents. I will briefly discuss two examples to make this point clear. One is the sign of a golf school in Gotanda (got040). The information that this is a golf school is provided in both Japanese (*gorufu sukūru*) and English. Non-overlapping is the name of the school, which is given only in a Romanised version within the English line 'KAWANAMI GOLF SCHOOL' and Japanese-only information that the school is situated in the basement of 'this building' (*tōbiru* B1). Again, the pragmatic details (spatial deixis) are confined to the Japanese version.

The second example is a price list of a beauty parlour in Tabata (tab025). The relatively large amount of text on the sign is almost completely non-overlapping: the title of the sign ('menu'), the name of the business, and its opening hours are given in English; all services and prices in Japanese. The only piece of information available in both languages is the day on which the business is closed, 'SUNDAY' and, in brackets, *nichi*. As these two cases exemplify, there is considerable variation as regards the amount of non-overlapping information on mixed signs of this type, suggesting rather complex profiles of the targeted group of readers.

With regard to the reasons for being multilingual rather than mono-lingual signs it is much less evident that mixed signs of the latter two types have been produced in order to make a message available in another language in addition to Japanese. The languages on many of these signs are intended to fulfil complementary rather than supple-mentary functions. In this respect they are much more akin to the group of polyphonic signs, to which we will turn next.

## Polyphonic signs

Polyphonic signs contain several languages or Japanese glosses completely independent of each other in content. In other words, one version does not give away any information contained in the respective co-appearing version. The two examples in Figures 5.6 and 5.7 demonstrate this. One is the sign of a hairdresser's in Harajuku (har012). It gives most of the information in English only: the name and the nature of the business, its opening hours, and where it allegedly comes from. However, there is also one piece of not too trivial information available only in Japanese. It says that the salon is closed on Tuesdays. Since no information is given in both languages, the full content of the sign can be properly understood only by someone with a minimal proficiency in both Japanese and English.

The second example, a litter box outside a convenience store in Tabata (tab035), requires a bilingual reader, too. The two languages give very different kinds of information. While the English text reminds us that garbage separation is important to 'SAVE THE EARTH', the Japanese text contains more specific information about how this can possibly be done. It determines what type of garbage is to be put into which box. Were it not for the supplementary pictograms given below the Japanese text, proficiency in English would be useless in order to understand that this is a litter box reserved for (glass) bottles and cans. The choice of the two languages in either example follows a characteristic pattern. Whereas Japanese is used to convey everyday matters such as opening hours or details about garbage separation, English deals with more global issues – that the hairdresser comes from abroad, for instance, and that it is important to save the planet.

Similar patterns of functional distribution are found on many other polyphonic signs. Prototypical examples are cigarette advertisements that use English slogans like 'SLOW DOWN. PLEASURE UP.' (yoy023, sbu055, etc.) or 'Come to where the flavor is' (sug137, tam034, etc.). The accompanying warning that smoking is detrimental to one's health, however, is given in Japanese. A great number of signs exhibit comparable functional distributions in combining English slogans and catch-phrases such as 'Unwire your Life' (aki020) and 'Have a good time' (sug046) or business names such as 'Lady's Fashion SHIRAYURI' (kom078) and 'Hair Studio KOTAKA' (tab018) with more specific information in Japanese.

Another pattern frequently found on polyphonic signs is the use of an English title such as 'Information' (aki031), 'floor Guide' (tab013), 'PRICE LIST' (sju001), or 'Beauty Menu' (tab022) on signs that give all subsequent information announced by that title in Japanese only. It is obvious that the information value of this type of sign is relatively low

**Figure 5.6** Sign at a hairdresser's (har012)

**Figures 5.7** Text on a litter box (tab035)

to anyone knowing English but not Japanese. One may go so far as to claim that many of these titles themselves are not English words but merely English spellings of Japanese borrowings, represented in the script and the spelling of their donor language. We will come back to this point in 5.9.

Yet another prominent type of polyphonic sign is signs containing Japanese–English mixed names of shops, companies, restaurants, and other businesses, for instance: 'COFFEE & RESTAURANT *jonasan*' [Jonathan] (ugu033), 'Mansion & Hotel *sezāru*' [César] (meg032), or 'GAME *rasubegasu*' [Las Vegas] (sbu060) (see also Table 5.30 on p. 125). A possible motivation for these frequently found instances of code-mixing could be the desire to have foreign elements in a commercial name, while at the same time make sure that the Japanese background of the business is recognisable. Another reason might be that the apparently foreign elements on these signs have not been considered foreign by the sign writer at all (see 5.9).

Table 5.20 gives the proportions of the three types of polyphonic signs. The total number of items is 340, of which more than 40% exhibit a functional distribution between Japanese for everyday contents and English for more global matters. Around 20% of the signs each make use of an English title or display a Japanese-English mixed business name. In total, over 85% of the polyphonic signs can be classified as one of the three types.

It is safe to assume that signs in polyphonic style are multilingual signs made for the Japanese population. The fact that English and English-looking expressions are used mainly for slogans, catch-phrases, business names, and titles suggests a general demand for signs containing some foreign elements. As soon as it comes to information of a more specific or more complicated nature, however, the language switches to Japanese. To people without proficiency in Japanese this information is inaccessible.

**Table 5.20** Types of polyphonic signs

| *Pattern* | *Cases* | % |
|---|---|---|
| Global (E) vs. everyday (J) contents | 145 | 42.6 |
| English title vs. Japanese contents | 69 | 20.3 |
| Mixed business name | 76 | 22.4 |
| Others | 50 | 14.7 |
| **Sum** | **340** | **100** |

## Monophonic signs

Monophonic signs are signs with only one language or Japanese gloss. Three basic types can be distinguished: (1) single word signs such as 'SALE' (ike001), 'Open' (got034), or 'WELCOME' (sbu143); (2) signs displaying brief slogans and catchphrases, for instance 'Security & Safety' (ebi045; see 5.10) or 'We make a difference in quality and freshness' (meg069); and (3) signs giving names of shops ('SHOES HAGIMOTO' (oka025), 'Textile Boutique TAKATOMI' (kan050)), companies ('FACTORY NAGATA' (kom112), 'T. SONODA ARCHITECTS & ENGINEERS, INC.' (yoy017)), or products ('Asahi Soft Drinks' (tab056), 'SUNTORY COFFEE' (sug147)). As shown in Table 5.21, more than 80% of all monophonic items belong to one of the three types.

Most of these signs are of a similar nature to polyphonic signs. They merely differ in that, since more specific or complicated information is not included, no shift to Japanese is necessary. The main target group is the Japanese-speaking population, though people not knowing Japanese may profit from the signs as well.

A closer look at how the languages and Japanese glosses are distributed within the four categories substantiates the above assumptions. Table 5.22 gives the distributions for the 2433 valid cases of the sample. It should not come as a surprise that monophonic and polyphonic signs are almost exclusively English or Japanese–English signs, with 97.9% each. This is the one foreign language most people in Japan can be expected to make some sense of even without translation, particularly when presented in such a spoon-fed way (single words, catch-phrases, etc.) as discussed above. Only 13 monophonic and 10 polyphonic signs contain foreign languages other than English: Chinese (2 items), Korean (10 items), French (9 items), and Portuguese (2 items). For the signs containing French text a similar point can be made as for the majority of English-only signs. They are commercial signs with very short texts, partially mentioned already in section 5.3: 'HABITATION FORÊT' (ugu023), 'PÂTISSIER INAMURA SHOZO' (ugu053–057), and 'Salon de Thé Colombin' (har086–088).

**Table 5.21** Types of monophonic signs

| Pattern | Case | % |
|---|---|---|
| Single word | 141 | 23.0 |
| Slogan or catchphrase | 156 | 25.4 |
| Businesses name, etc. | 226 | 36.8 |
| Others | 91 | 14.8 |
| **Sum** | **614** | **100** |

**Table 5.22** Part writing type vs. languages/Japanese glosses

| Languages/J. glosses | Homoph. (n = 638) | Mixed (n = 841) | Polyph. (n = 340) | Monoph. (n = 614) |
|---|---|---|---|---|
| Japanese | | | | |
|   in Kanji & Kana | 97.6% | 97.9% | 94.7% | |
|   in Roman alphabet | 9.9% | 13.2% | 14.7% | |
|   with Furigana | 6.6% | 3.7% | | |
|   in Braille | 1.6% | 1.2% | | |
| English | 88.4% | 90.0% | 97.9% | 97.9% |
| Chinese | 0.8% | 6.5% | 0.6% | |
| Korean | 0.8% | 3.0% | 0.9% | 1.1% |
| French | 1.3% | 1.5% | 0.7% | |
| Portuguese | 0.2% | 1.1% | | 0.3% |
| Spanish | 0.2% | 0.8% | | |
| Latin | | 0.7% | | |
| Thai | | 0.6% | | |
| Italian | | 0.5% | | |
| Persian | | 0.2% | | |
| Tagalog | | 0.2% | | |
| German | | 0.2% | | |
| Arabic | | 0.1% | | |
| Russian | 0.2% | | | |

The monophonic and polyphonic signs in Chinese, Korean, and Portuguese are different in nature. The texts are much longer and in most cases provide concrete and quite specified information about available goods and services (e.g. got004–005, sok003, sok035, sok083–085, tak061–062). One example is a handwritten Portuguese sign attached to the window of a photo studio in the area in Gotanda (got004). It contains the following text:

FOTOS PARA PASSAPORTE BRASILEIRO E ALISTAMENTO MILITAR.
EMPRESTAMOS PALETÓ E GRAVATA

This message is not intended to be understood by the ordinary Japanese passer-by, to whom it would be of little use to know that photos for Brazilian passports and for signing up in the military are available here. The text on the sign is to be read by Portuguese-speaking Brazilians on their way to the Brazilian consulate around the corner (see 5.3). Alongside the few monophonic and polyphonic Chinese and Korean signs, the example constitutes a rare but important exception to the common pattern of information provision found on this type of sign. All other foreign languages do not appear without supplementary translation at all. Their absence from monophonic and polyphonic signs implies that they are not expected to be understood by any sizeable number of speakers in Tokyo.

Some other observations about the four types of part writing can be made with regard to the official or non-official background of a sign. A cross tabulation of the two variables is given in Table 5.23. Almost all signs without mutual translations or transliterations are bottom-up, that is, non-official signs. Only 16 top-down signs have been identified as monophonic or polyphonic signs. The distribution of mixed signs is more equally balanced, with around 60% bottom-up vs. 40% top-down signs. For the group of homophonic signs there are even slightly more top-down (53.1%) than bottom-up signs (46.9%). In other words, multilingual signs not providing mutual translations or transliterations are almost exclusively set up by non-official agents. The more information is made available in more than one language (or Japanese gloss) the more likely it becomes that the sign has an official originator. With regard to the target group of the four types of signs, this outcome suggests that official signs are made multilingual in order to be of use to people with non-Japanese backgrounds. Non-official multilingual signs do not necessarily have this aim. In many cases they address a predominantly Japanese readership.

In conclusion, a closer look at part writing patterns of multilingual signs has proved helpful to sort out different types of signs serving different kinds of functions. A basic rule of thumb is as follows: whenever a translation or transliteration is available, the sign has been designed in a multilingual format with people of foreign backgrounds in mind, whereas the absence of translation or transliteration means that the sign is a multilingual sign made for the Japanese population. Homophonic and most mixed signs are of the former type, polyphonic and monophonic signs of the latter. This rule holds for the majority of signs in the sample, but not for all. Monophonic signs in languages other than English or French, for instance, seem to address a foreign rather

**Table 5.23** Part writing type vs. top-down/bottom-up

| Type of sign | Homoph. (n = 638) | Mixed (n = 841) | Polyph. (n = 340) | Monoph. (n = 614) |
|---|---|---|---|---|
| Top-down | 53.1% | 41.1% | 0.3% | 2.4% |
| Bottom-up | 46.9% | 58.9% | 99.7% | 97.6% |

than a Japanese target group, whereas the sign writer of a mixed sign with overlapping information arrangement is likely to have had a Japanese rather than a foreign target group in mind. Yet another group of signs constituting an exception to the rule will be identified in the next section.

## 5.7 Code Preference

This section takes a closer look at visual hierarchies of languages and Japanese glosses on the signs of the sample. Since it is hardly practicable to display more than one message on the same piece of space – an exception being combinations of print and Braille texts, a choice must be made as to which of two or more messages is to appear in prominent position. This choice inevitably produces a visual hierarchy. Moreover, it suggests a direction of translation (or transliteration) in making the text given in prominent position appear as the original version from which the co-appearing other versions are derived. Using the terminology suggested by Scollon and Scollon (2003; see 3.7), I will refer to this issue as 'code preference'.

Scollon and Scollon distinguish three types of code preference. The two most frequent ways of expressing a hierarchy are order and font size, referred to by Cenoz and Gorter (2006; see 3.4) as 'first language' and 'size of text', respectively. A third option is giving the languages on separate signs set up at different points in space, a practice to be discussed in section 5.8. Previous research has mainly focused on the order of the languages (Spolsky & Cooper, 1991; Wenzel, 1996). It goes without saying that what is intended to appear as original can be assumed to come first. Since Japanese is a language customarily written both in a horizontal vector from left to right and in a vertical vector from right to left, code preference is given to the version of a message positioned on top (in horizontal text) or on the right (in vertical text).

I partially deviate here from Scollon and Scollon (2003: 120; see 3.7), who consider the preferred code to be exclusively on top, on the left, or in the centre of a sign. In view of the Chinese-based script tradition in East Asia, it is justified to assume a reversed, that is, right–left order of preference for multilingual signs with a vertical text vector. Kress and van Leeuwen (1996: 199), on whose approach Scollon and Scollon base their considerations, themselves acknowledge that their framework is 'largely concerned with the description of the visual semiotic of Western cultures. Cultures which have long-established reading directions of different kind (right to left or top to bottom) are likely to attach different values to these positions' (see also Jewitt & Oyama, 2001).

The two street block signs in Figures 5.8 and 5.9 demonstrate this point. The sign from Chiyoda Ward (yur014) follows the top-down

**Figure 5.8** Street block sign (yur014)

**Figure 5.9** Street block sign (uen017)

principle, whereas the one from Taitō Ward (uen017) is organised from right to left. In either case the Japanese version can be easily recognised as coming first. In some cases, these differing script conventions allow the organisation of the encounter of Japanese and Western languages in a way that neither version will appear to be preferred. For instance, a map in the area in Uguisudani (ugu007) gives the horizontal English version of its title on top and the vertical Japanese version on the right. Each version then, according to the respective script conventions, appears in first position.

Even more important for the visual impression of a multilingual sign is the size of the texts. What is supposed to be the original version can be assumed to be the one that has been assigned the most space. In the majority of cases, size and position imply the same ranking. The version assigned preferential status covers the largest space and is given on top (or on the right hand). In cases where size and order do not express the same preference, size can be considered to outweigh order (Scollon & Scollon, 2003: 125).

Two examples are given in Figures 5.10 and 5.11. On the commercial sign found in Akihabara (aki075) the larger Japanese text can be considered to be the original, while the smaller English version, though positioned on top, appears as translation. The same applies to signs in a vertical text vector, such as the second example. The sign gives the name of a slope in the Shibuya area (sbu045). Though the Romanised transliteration precedes the Japanese Kanji version in order, the size of the two texts indicates that the latter is supposed to be the original.

The present analysis is confined to signs with texts constituting complete or partial translations or transliterations of each other. Of all 1479 items classified as homophonic or mixed signs (see 5.6), code preference could be determined for 1311 items. The residuary 168 signs could not be categorised for various reasons: because no photos were available (mainly 'push/pull' tags, e.g. sbu163–171); because separate carriers were used (e.g. tok005; see 5.8); because the different versions were given in constant repetition on electric sign boards (e.g. sok013) or on round carriers (e.g. kom115); because the sign did not contain a Japanese version (e.g. sok096); because the two codes contained were Japanese in Kanji & Kana and Japanese in Furigana (e.g. ugu078); or because preference was given more than once to different codes (e.g. tam055).

The 1311 items for which a determination of code preference was possible have been categorised as translating or transliterating either from or into Japanese. Code preference in the former case can be considered unmarked, while in the latter case it is marked. The quantitative results of the analysis are given in Table 5.24. As one might expect, for the overall majority of signs (80.2%) code preference is unmarked, that is, given to the Japanese version. This tendency is more salient for

**Figure 5.10** Commercial sign (aki075)

**Figure 5.11** Toponymic sign (sbu045)

**Table 5.24** Code preference on mixed and homophonic signs

| Code preference | Mixed signs (n = 811) | Homoph. signs (n = 500) | Sum (n = 1311) |
|---|---|---|---|
| Unmarked | 71.9% | 93.8% | 80.2% |
| Marked | 28.1% | 6.2% | 19.8% |
| Sum | 100% | 100% | 100% |

homophonic signs (93.8%) than for mixed signs (71.9%). The visual impression of unmarked code preference is that a supplementary translation or transliteration from Japanese in Kanji & Kana into a foreign language or Japanese gloss is given. Coming back to the question formulated in 5.6, such signs suggest that they have a multilingual design in order to be comprehensible to people with limited or no Japanese reading proficiency. All examples given in this section so far have been such cases.

Of special interest are the residuary approximately 20% signs of marked code preference, that is, signs on which the non-Japanese version is displayed in prominent position. Two examples of this type of sign are given in Figures 5.12 and 5.13. The first item is a mixed sign of a dance school in Sugamo (sug032). The English name of the school, 'M's DANCE ACADEMY', is followed by a Katakana transliteration into *emuzu dansu akademī*. The second example, a homophonic sign of a picture gallery in Okachimachi (oka026), shows the same characteristics. Again there is an English business name subsequently transliterated into Katakana. In either case both size and order underline that the English version is the original from which the Japanese one has been derived.

In quantitative terms, homophonic and mixed signs of this type make up 10.6% of the 2444 signs of the sample. These signs are instances of foreign language use that deserve special attention. They visually exemplify that a multilingual sign is not necessarily the result of a translation (or transliteration) from Japanese into another language (or Japanese gloss) but that it can be exactly the other way round. A multilingual sign may be produced out of need to make a message originally conveyed in a foreign language available in Japanese, too. The sole function of the Japanese version is to provide a reading aid, in a similar way that Furigana annotations for difficult Kanji characters do (Coulmas, 1999: 14–15). In such cases it appears as though it were the monolingual parts of the Japanese population who are in need of linguistic support, rather than any group of foreign minorities.

There are two possible explanations for this. One likely reason is that the sign writer has a foreign background. A characteristic example of

**Figure 5.12** Sign of a dance school (sug032)

**Figure 5.13** Sign of a picture gallery (oka026)

this type of marked code preference is menus of Chinese restaurants that give the Chinese name of each dish before the corresponding Japanese version (e.g. tak041, ham038, sin011). With regard to the terminology discussed in Chapter 4, this way of code preference would be indexical in that it relates to the linguistic origin of the business the sign stands for.

The other possible reason for marked code preference is that the sign is to imply a foreign background that actually does not exist. Particularly with regard to English texts, marked code preference on a considerable number of signs seems to be motivated by this second reason. Code preference in these cases could be considered symbolic rather than indexical in that, as Scollon and Scollon (2003: 133) have pointed out, it is based on something 'which is not present or which is ideal or metaphorical'. A similar point could be made for many of the monophonic multilingual signs discussed in section 5.6. The only difference is that preference of the non-Japanese code in this latter case is not expressed by size or order but by the simple fact that a Japanese version is not available at all.

A look at possible correlations between code preference and the top-down/bottom-up variable reveals that marked code preference is a practice almost exclusively reserved to non-official signs. As shown in Table 5.25, only six of the 662 official signs (0.9%) display a language other than Japanese in prominent position. This reflects what official documents about sign writing provide for. For instance, the Metropolitan Government's *Tokyo Manual about Official Signs* of 1991 determines that 'the size of the English text is half that of the corresponding Japanese text' (TMG, 1991: 36) and the 2003 *Guide for Making City Writing Easy to Understand Also to Foreigners* specifies that 'an interlinear order with Japanese above and Rōmaji below is desirable' (TMG, 2003: 9). The 1994 *Shinagawa Ward Basic Manual about Street Signs* is even more specific:

> For the English text, half the size of the Japanese text is considered standard ... Rather than strict factual half-size it is important that the visually perceived size is felt to be half that of the Japanese size. (Shinagawa Ward, 1994: 32)

Bottom-up signs are much less eager to give Japanese in prominent position, with less than 60% complying with the above regulations. Giving an impression of foreignness – real or fake – thus seems to be desirable only for signs of a non-official nature. Official agents try to avoid the impression that the sign writer could be anything but Japanese.

In summary, this section has shown that the great majority of analysable signs assign a predominant role to the Japanese version of a message. This trend is particularly salient for signs of an official origin, which almost without exception are unmarked in code preference. On

**Table 5.25** Code preference vs. top-down/bottom-up

| Code preference | Top-down signs (n = 662) | Bottom-up signs (n = 649) |
|---|---|---|
| Unmarked | 99.1% | 61.0% |
| Marked | 0.9% | 39.0% |
| **Sum** | **100%** | **100%** |

the other hand, we have also seen that a sizeable number of non-official signs give the non-Japanese version as the preferred code. No matter whether this preference is considered indexical or symbolic – a problem to which we will come back in the general conclusions in Chapter 6, these signs visually question the predominant role of Japanese in the streets of Tokyo. In this respect, signs of marked code preference are indicative of ongoing changes in the city's linguistic landscape.

## 5.8 Visibility

Multilingual information on signs can come in two ways: either on one sign containing two or more languages or on several signs containing one language each. In the former case the multilingual nature of a sign is visible at first sight; in the latter it is not. This difference with regard to visibility is included as one variable in Reh's (2004; see 3.6) typology of multilingual signs. In her study in Lira Town she makes an overall distinction between overt and covert forms of written multilingualism. If different versions of a text are contained on one carrier, the multilingual nature of the sign is overt; if they are given on separate carriers, it is covert.

In order to determine the frequency of non-visible multilingual signs in the 28 survey areas, it was necessary to work with some additional data. In the course of the survey I recorded also Japanese-only signs that were not classified as multilingual but that had corresponding multilingual counterparts with the same design. Most of these signs, which are not part of the 2444 survey items, were set up in close proximity to their non-Japanese equivalents. Often they were attached to the same carrier. It should be specified therefore that the term 'visibility' as employed here merely refers to the display of texts either within one single frame or within separate frames. Due to the underlying definition of the term 'sign' as given in 5.1, the defining boundary is the frame of a sign rather than its carrier. The fact that texts within separate frames may be simultaneously visible is not taken into consideration.

As became evident during data collection, non-visible multilingual signs are a rather exceptional sight in Tokyo. In total, only 28 items were found to display their contents in separate frames. A sub-categorisation shows that signs providing translations or transliterations in separate frames are usually attached next to each other. The example in Figure 5.14 is such a case. The two signs belong to a fashion shop in Harajuku (har050 and har+01). The same message is given on two separate signs in English and Japanese, respectively.

A second way of multilingual information provision within separate frames is making use of the front and back of a carrier. A rotating sign-board in Ōsaki (osa006 and osa+01), for instance, prohibits the parking of cars. As can be seen in Figures 5.15 and 5.16, the message is given in Japanese on one side of the carrier and in English on the other. The sign can easily be mistaken for a monolingual sign, either in Japanese or English. Whatever viewpoint one chooses, each language is visible only when the other is not.

A mixture of the two types of non-visible multilingual signs is a series of three posters attached to the glass entrance door of a telephone shop in Gotanda (got007–009). The posters inform the users of a certain type of prepaid cellular phone that the product will soon become obsolete and needs to be exchanged. The message is given in English, Russian,

**Figure 5.14** Two signs at the entrance of a boutique (har050 and har+01)

**Figure 5.15** No-Parking sign, front (osa006)

**Figure 5.16** No-Parking sign, back (osa+01)

and Portuguese in identical versions within separate frames attached close to each other. The back of each of the signs contained still another language: Japanese, Chinese, and Korean, respectively. However, since the backs were visible only from inside the shop, they were considered to be outside the survey area and therefore not included in the sample. The three counted items are given in Figure 5.17.

The majority of the 28 non-visible multilingual signs were found attached not too far from each other and facing the same direction (Figure 5.14). On six signs the front and back of a carrier were made use of (Figures 5.15 and 5.16). The three signs given in Figure 5.17 can be allocated to either category. The results are summarised in Table 5.26.

**Table 5.26** Multilingual signs in separate frames

| Mode of display | Cases | Figure no. |
|---|---|---|
| Next to each other | 19 | 5.14 |
| Front and back | 6 | 5.15, 5.16 |
| Both | 3 | 5.17 |
| **Sum** | **28** | |

**Figure 5.17** Three posters at a telephone shop (got007–009)

The main advantage of conveying a multilingual message in the form of separate, apparently monolingual, signs is the avoidance of code preference (see 5.7). If two or more versions of a text come within separate frames, the signs usually provide no clue about linguistic hierarchies (see also Hannahs, 1989: 57–8). However, Scollon and Scollon (2003; see 3.7) have emphasised that a sign obtains an important part of its meaning from being situated in physical space. Even if two or more versions of a sign are given in separate frames, their emplacement may suggest a ranking order.

The 28 items of the Tokyo sample support this view. Though the messages come in separate frames, there are several ways of indicating code preference. For instance, one can attach one version of a message on top of its co-occurring counterpart (sok038, ebi018, etc.). In addition, at least three other ways of indicating code preference are practised: (1) 'front vs. back', that is, signs like the above-mentioned telephone shop's posters, whose fronts are directed towards the street while the backs are visible only from inside the shop (got007–009; also kom080); (2) 'close vs. remote', that is, signs at unequal distances from the reader's presumed viewpoint (e.g. sok025, har050); and (3) 'earlier vs. later', that is, signs coming into sight earlier or later with regard to the reader's assumed direction of movement (e.g. tok005, tok024, tok027).

In general, however, it must be re-emphasised that the use of separate frames is rare in linguistic landscaping in Tokyo. The overwhelming majority of multilingual signs give the two or more versions of a message within the same frame. Their multilingual nature is revealed at first sight, even to people not knowing all of the languages and scripts contained. This is important to know because, as discussed in Chapter 4, the visibility or non-visibility of multilingualism has implications for the general attitudes towards the linguistic make-up of a city on the part of its inhabitants. On commercial signs in and around Brussels, for instance, corresponding messages in French and Dutch are for the most part given on separate signs rather than co-appearing. As pointed out in section 3.1, the separation of the two languages can be interpreted as an expression of lingering linguistic conflict between Flemish and Walloons in the Belgian capital.

In contrast to the situation in Brussels, the appearance of several languages within the same frame does not seem to constitute a problem in Tokyo. It goes without saying that a direct comparison of the two cities is problematic. Tokyo is not a traditionally bilingual city, and there is no other major language group apart from the Japanese. Moreover, as the analysis in the previous sections has shown, a considerable number of signs containing languages other than Japanese address a predominantly Japanese readership. Use of a foreign language therefore is not necessarily intended to be a concession to any other language group.

**Figure 5.18** Public order poster (har042)

**Figure 5.19** Poster of a paint shop (sbu144)

It often simply follows an apparent demand by the host population for a multilingual outward appearance of their city. The scarcity of non-visible multilingual signs shows that visibility of multilingualism is desired and fully intended in Tokyo.

The popularity of visibly multilingual signs is most salient on signs that do not provide translations or transliterations but whose symmetric design suggests that they would. Two examples of this type of sign are given in Figures 5.18 and 5.19. Judging only from their design, one may get the impression that the two items are Japanese–English signs giving translations of each other. In either case, however, the English version has little in common with the Japanese one. The first example, a public order poster in Harajuku (har042), contains two messages. The one on the left is from a public primary school, whose name is given at the bottom left of the sign. The message by the school's pupils is 'We love the town that we were born in. We love the town that brought us up'. It is unrelated to the corresponding English appeal to 'keep clean, keep green' on the right-hand side of the poster, whose originator is a local shopkeepers' association.

The second example is a poster in the window of a paint shop in Shibuya (sbu144). Again the design of the poster would suggest that the English text above the '2003' in the centre is a translation of the Japanese text below, or vice versa. Though this may have been the intention by the sign writer, the English version, unlike the Japanese one, is for the most part incomprehensible. It is given on the poster not in order to convey the contents of a message, but because the sign writer must have assumed that an apparently bilingual format would be more appealing to the general public than a monolingual Japanese one. It is almost as though the sign would have remained somehow incomplete unless given in a bilingual design.

Both examples are make-believe translations. They contain English not in order to make a message understandable to people not knowing Japanese, but simply because, as this section has shown, visibility of multilingualism is highly appreciated in Tokyo.

## 5.9 Idiosyncrasies

Caution! Don't lean on the gate. The gate would fall down when lean on it. It occurs you Trouble. (Electronic gate to prevent shoplifting, sbu010)

CROSS LINKING ARTISTS AND MATERIAL DRIVE FOR ART OF POLYMERZAION AND GROW TOGETHER. (Paint shop, sbu144; see Figure 5.19)

> The Italian word "Pomodoro" means "Golden fruit". It seems that when the givin name in old days, tomatoes were of a yellow color. Tomatoes have vitamin, carotene, potash, pectene? [*sic*] and is good for blood pressure, liver desease, and constipation. An old European proverb goes "doctors turn pale when tomatoes turn red". This synbolizes why tomatoes were called a golden fruit, not only for their color. (Italian restaurant, sbu145)

These are some rather extraordinary cases of foreign language use found in the survey area in Shibuya. While similar examples have recently aroused some interest from art photographers (Larsen, 1993), in popular literature (Evens, 2000; Jerome, 1997), and on websites (e.g. www. engrish.com), this study is not intended to contribute to the increasing body of collections of funniest, stupidest, Japlish, Jenglish, whatever, signs. However, linguistic idiosyncrasies – in English as in other languages – constitute an integral part of the signs of the sample that should not be ignored altogether. They will be dealt with in this section.

Generally speaking, there is a different degree of tolerance towards deviation from what is considered 'proper' language use in the written mode than there is in the oral mode. This is due to the essentially different nature of the medium. As discussed in section 2.2, speech is bound to the time of utterance and, therefore, evanescent. A message in the written mode, by contrast, is permanent, and any kind of idiosyncrasy remains observable long after it has been produced.

On a terminological note, 'idiosyncrasy' is used here in order to avoid expressions such as 'error' or 'mistake'. The present purpose is not to evaluate whether the text on a given sign is 'right' or 'wrong', provided such a clear-cut distinction was possible at all. Rather, it is to examine what types of idiosyncrasies can be identified and how they can be interpreted. It will be shown that many of the examples result from interference from one language or writing system on the other. We will concentrate on texts in the four most frequent languages: (1) English, (2) Japanese, and (3) Chinese and Korean.

## English

Being the most frequent foreign language overall, English accounts for the majority of idiosyncrasies. A first point already mentioned en passant in section 5.2 is double representations on toponymic signs. Examples are 'Kototoi dōri Ave.' [lit. Kototoi Street Avenue] (ugu013), 'Zojoji Temple' [lit. Zōjō Temple Temple] (ham048), and 'Rikugien Garden' [lit. Rikugi Garden Garden] (kom005), among many others. As a look at administrative guidelines about sign writing shows, this is an officially promoted strategy. For instance, the 1991 *Tokyo Manual about Official*

*Signs* by the Metropolitan Government (TMG, 1991: 17) provides that 'in cases where one cannot sever common nouns from conventionalised proper nouns, the whole expression is given in Rōmaji with English . . . added where necessary'. Similarly, recent guidelines by the Ministry of Land, Infrastructure and Transport recommend that 'when an expression consists of a proper noun only, it is desirable that an English term conveying the meaning should be supplemented, such as "~Bridge" or "~River"' (MLIT/EcoMo, 2001: 37; MLIT/EcoMo, 2002: 16). Though the occurrence of double representations on toponymic signs hence appears to be the result of official language planning, it remains a rather idiosyncratic practice to anyone with at least some proficiency in both English and Japanese.

A further factor regularly producing idiosyncrasies is use and non-use of upper case letters. There are several signs where capital letters appear within coherent phrases, for instance, 'Chinese wine and Soft drinks' on a menu in Shinagawa (sna007). They occasionally even occur within single words such as 'for ChinZansō', a place name on a bus stop in Mejiro (mio034), where the intra-word capital – intentionally or not – marks a phoneme boundary. On the other hand, use of the lower case at the beginning of a phrase, such as in 'floor Guide' (tab013), is not a rare sight either. Particularly in the commercial domain, however, such deviation from common orthographic practices may be fully intentional rather than a result of carelessness or lack in proficiency.

Other orthographic idiosyncrasies are more striking. For instance, in the domain of eating and drinking we find examples such as 'Alcohl' (ike052), 'side ordar' (got013), 'chickin' (got035), and even a 'Chainese restaurant' (tab011), whereas shops dealing in fashion and beauty write terms like 'Accusesari' (har085), 'INPORT' (sbu002), and 'Parm' (meg040) on their signs. Regarding the fact that many of the terms in question have become part of the Japanese lexicon and now coexist as Japanese borrowings, it is easy to recognise these orthographic idiosyncrasies as results of interference. That is, their spelling is influenced by the way they would be spelled when re-transliterated from their borrowed Japanese Katakana offspring. Table 5.27 gives a list of examples. Whether interference occurs on the graphemic or on the phonemic level is hard to tell – probably a combination of both.

Idiosyncrasies can also be observed on the morphosyntactic level. The most striking characteristic is missing plural inflections. This type of idiosyncrasy is found not only on all sorts of commercial bottom-up signs offering 'HOME MADE BURGER AND CAKE' (ots030), 'cocktail' (sok090), 'DRUG & COSMETIC' (sju029), or 'cigarette' (osa106), but on top-down signs as well. For instance, information plates on postboxes explain which of the two slots is to be used for 'LETTER POSTCARD' (e.g. yoy010, got023). Similar inscriptions can be found on recycling boxes

**Table 5.27** Examples of orthographic interference

| Survey number | Original English term | Japanese loan | Transliteration | Spelling on sign |
|---|---|---|---|---|
| har085 | accessory | アクセサリー | *akusesarī* | accusesari |
| ike052 | alcohol | アルコール | *arukōru* | alcohl |
| meg040 | blow | ブロー | *burō* | brow |
| got035 | chicken | チキン | *chikin* | chickin |
| tab011 | Chinese | チャイニーズ | *chainīzu* | Chainese |
| ebi015 | cocktails | カクテル | *kakuteru* | cacktails |
| sok080 | hamburger steak | ハンバーグ | *hanbāgu* | hamburg |
| sbu002 | import | インポート | *inpōto* | inport |
| meg040 | perm | パーマ | *pāma* | parm |
| got013 | side order | サイドオーダー | *saido ōdā* | side ordar |
| got013 | strawberry | ストロベリー | *sutoroberī* | storawberry |

separating 'GLASS BOTTLE' from 'CAN' (kom068). Absence of plural endings is almost symptomatic on signs about opening hours, for instance 'Weekday am10:00~pm8:00' (kom060) and 'Sunday & Holiday 9:00~19:00' (ots038). Sometimes the plural is marked as though it was a genitive singular, as in '7 day's open' (har048).

Inflectional idiosyncrasies, though to a lesser degree, can also be observed for agreement of the verb phrase. Thus there is a warning that all bicycles left in the area around Ikebukuro station 'will be impound in accordance with TOSIMA CITY Ordinance' (e.g. ike025; see the quotation in 5.5 on p. 87). In a similar way a sign outside a hairdresser informs us that the business is 'close SUNDAY' (tab025). A third example, where inflectional idiosyncrasies of the verb phrase result in a rather weird, though formally correct, sentence is 'THIS STORE ELECTRONICALLY PROTECTED AGAINST SHOPLIFTING' (sok038, ebi010).

Yet another morphosyntactic idiosyncrasy concerns determiners. For instance, a major clothes manufacturing company whose head office is situated in Akihabara (aki049, aki112) uses the slogan 'DAIDOH – FOR THE HIGHER QUALITY IN LIFE'. Similar signs were found in Yoyogi (yoy001) and Ebisu (ebi007), where containers of fire extinguishers along the street bear the inscription 'A Fire Extinguisher' (see also 5.10). Most of these morphosyntactic idiosyncrasies can be interpreted as resulting from interference, since Japanese does not make use of determiners or inflections for number or person.

A third type of idiosyncrasy refers to the lexical level, where one frequently comes across rather unusual collocations such as 'Meet together and enjoy our Golf-Style' (oka48) or 'SERIOUS FITNESS FOR EVERY BODY' (har055). In many cases the expressions used are felt idiosyncratic only when considered part of the English lexicon. When thought of as Japanese terms they seem less odd. One example is the term 'coffee' in expressions such as 'COFFEE & RESTAURANT' (ugu033) or 'Coffee G2' (sbu138), where what is referred to as 'coffee' is supposed to designate a café or coffee shop. A similar case is the use of the word 'snack'. In Gotanda (got047), for instance, a sign indicates a business named 'PUB&SNACK PEARL'. As in 'Coffee & Restaurant', the apparent semantic mismatch is only in English. In Japanese, where the term *sunakku* designates a bar or a night club, the combination is not idiosyncratic.

The same can be said of the term 'menu', which is frequently found as a title on signs enlisting the prices of services available at hairdressers and beauty parlours (e.g. tab022, tab025). Again this is a specific Japanese use, where *menyū* can refer to a selection of products and services nonrelated to eating and drinking. A final example is the term 'make' in the sense of 'make-up' (ebi051, osa048, etc.). Knowing that the Japanese borrowing *mēku* is a well-established expression in the domain of cosmetics, signs such as 'EARTH – HAIR & make' (osa039) or, as quoted elsewhere, 'MAKE FACIAL CUT' (Evens, 2000) will appear much less idiosyncratic (see also Horvat, 2000: 97). Table 5.28 gives a list of the terms discussed.

Thus one frequently comes across apparently English expressions that only make sense when read as Japanese. It is hard to clearly allocate these terms to one language. From a formal point of view (script and spelling) they look English, whereas from a functional point of view (context) they had better be considered to be Japanese. Counting these terms as English makes sense only in so far as they cannot be considered to be Romanised Japanese according to any of the common transliteration systems. In such a case we should have found terms like 'Sunakku', 'Menyū', and 'Mēku', which however did not show up anywhere. Choice by the sign writer was always made in favour of the

**Table 5.28** Examples of lexical interference

| Survey number | English term given on sign | Corresponding Japanese term (transliteration) | English paraphrase |
|---|---|---|---|
| ugu033 | coffee | コーヒー (*kōhī*) | coffee shop, café |
| got047 | snack | スナック (*sunakku*) | night club, bar |
| tab022 | menu | メニュー (*menyū*) | price list |
| ebi051 | make | メーク (*mēku*) | make-up |

original English term, irrespective of the fact that the meaning of the term as used in Japanese deviates from English usage. It is only by virtue of this semantic deviation that one becomes aware that what appears as English with regard to script and spelling has to a certain extent become part of the Japanese language.

The same applies to many other English-looking terms that coexist with Japanese borrowings. Honna (1995: 54) has referred to this practice as 'the simple rewriting' of a Katakana expression, emphasising that 'what is written in the Roman alphabet is not (at least theoretically) supposed to be an English phrase'. Examples from the sample are 'GAME' (kan064), 'PC SHOP' (aki044), 'SALE!' (oka003), 'TICKET' (ike080), and 'Information' (aki031), to name but a few. That they should be read as Japanese is not so obvious because no idiosyncrasies with regard to English usage can be observed. Seen in this light, rewriting appears to be a common practice when representing Japanese borrowings in Roman script.

In general, a closer analysis of idiosyncratic uses of English on the signs of the sample reveals that many cases can be explained as resulting from interference. This interpretation is particularly convincing with regard to spelling and lexicon, but has some explanatory force when it comes to morphosyntactic idiosyncrasies as well.

## Japanese

Japanese texts on the signs of the sample exhibit various forms of linguistic idiosyncrasies, too. Note that some of these texts by themselves have not been considered relevant to classify a sign as multilingual but happened to become part of the sample because they co-appeared on signs that for other reasons were counted as multilingual. We will start with idiosyncrasies concerning the use of Braille.

Braille was found on signs of postboxes in the areas in Tōkyō (tok036–039), Ikebukuro (ike044–047), Hamamatsuchō (ham044–047), and Shinbashi (sin052–055, sin056–059). Each postbox had attached to it four information plates in Japanese (in Kanji & Kana, in Braille, and, partially, with Furigana annotations) and English. The plates indicate which of the two slots is to be used for what type of mail. They also provide information about collection times, where to call in case of problems, etc. Idiosyncrasies of the Braille texts extend from slight variation in wording, a point to be discussed in section 5.10, to information substantially deviating from the corresponding print text. An example of the latter type is a plate on one of the two postboxes in Shinbashi (sin059). It names '11:50' as one of four collection times on weekdays, while the same information in the corresponding print version is '13:50'.

While most other information in Braille agreed with the meaning of the print text, there were some additional deficiencies on the Braille signs. Users of Braille criticised that it was often hard to read because it unnecessarily followed the design of the print text. For instance, the information on the plate about collection times was arranged in three columns, one for weekdays, one for Saturdays, and one for Sundays and holidays. While this is an organisation to follow by eye very easily, when read as Braille it is rather confusing because there is no indication of boundaries between the three columns. It was remarked that the sign would have been much easier to read if the information had been lined up within uninterrupted text.

Another point is that the Braille text contained slightly less information than the corresponding print text. This was observed for the plates about where to call in case of problems. Prefabricated text available on these plates in both (Japanese and English) print and Braille is *renrakusaki* ['Where to contact'], *denwa bangō* ['Telephone number'], and *posuto bangō* ['Name of this mailbox']. Specific information about these points, which has to be provided for each mailbox individually, is not given in Braille. Incidentally, it is not available in English either. In general, a closer examination of signs on postboxes reveals that, although the overall availability of information in Braille may be a helpful support to blind or visually disabled persons, many problems in detail remain to be solved (see also Hirose, 2005).

Other types of idiosyncrasies concern the transliteration of Japanese terms into the Roman alphabet. Syllabic /n/, for instance, when preceding <m>, <b>, or <p> is given alternatively as <n> and <m>. Such variation is particularly conspicuous when co-appearing in close proximity. One example is a bus stop in the area in Shinbashi, the name of which is indicated as 'Shimbashi-eki(Sta.)-kitaguchi' (sin026) on one sign, while it is given as 'SHINBASHI-EKI-KITAGUCHI' (sin027) on another. Similar variation is observable with regard to the use of <shi> or <si> for the same Kana symbol. While most transliterations use <shi> following the Hepburn transliteration system (see 3.10), the use of <si>, as proposed by the Kunrei system, is occasionally found, too. One example is a warning by the Toshima ward administration that a 'TOSIMA City Ordinance' prohibits leaving one's bicycle in no-parking areas (e.g. ike025; see 5.5). However, a similar sign by the same originator, this time referring to a 'Toshima City Ordinance', is also in use (kom050).

The situation is still more complex for the Romanisation of long vowels. The two most frequent representations of /o:/, for instance, are <ō>, as in 'Hanzōmon' (yur005), or simply <o>, as in 'Zojoji Temple' (ham048). In addition, at least three alternatives exist: the use of a cuneiform mark instead of a macron, as in 'RÂMEN FROM KYÔTO' (kom062); the attachment of <u>, as in 'HIP HOP WEAR Kinou' (osa042); and the attachment of <h>, as in 'GATE CITY OHSAKI' (osa010). Variation may even occur within one term, for instance in 'PHARMACY HŌSEIDO' (sok082), where both <ō> and <o> are long vowels that should be expected to be transliterated as either 'Hoseido' or 'Hōseidō'.

Finally, there are instances of ill-formed transliterations. Three cases were found in the area in Harajuku (har039–041) on the signs of a porcelain shop called 'HARAJYUKU TOGASHA'. Depending on which of the transliteration systems is followed, the Romanisation of the place name should be either 'Harajuku' (Hepburn) or 'Harazyuku' (Kunrei) but not, in any case, a blend of both, although such blends are reported to appear even on official government websites (e.g. Horvat, 2000: 165; Inoue, 2001: 187–8). In general, the above examples show that there is a great deal of inconsistency in the transliteration of Japanese terms in Tokyo's linguistic landscape.

Idiosyncrasies of a different type concern transliteration into the opposite direction, that is, the representation of borrowings and foreign terms in Japanese text. The ordinary way of integrating such terms is using the Katakana script. Their perceived overuse, commonly referred to as 'Katakana overflow', is a widely discussed issue in Japan that has been given ample attention in previous research and need not be discussed here (see Stanlaw, 2004: 11–14 for an overview; see also 3.10). A popular practice much less discussed so far is leaving foreign elements unchanged, that is, integrating them into Japanese text in their original script and spelling.

This type of code- and script-mixing is particularly prominent on the lexical level. Examples from the sample are '*naiyō wa* STAFF *made*' [For contents see staff] (meg033), '*ame no hi* 10% off' [On rainy days 10% off] (osa057), and '*suteki na* DESSERT SET' [Lovely dessert set] (sbu080). A frequent component in mixed expressions is the term 'or' used to enumerate products or services. Three examples are menus offering a chicken dish with '*raisu* or *pan*' [Rice or bread] (har022), a bagel that is '*purēn* or *shinamonrēzun*' [Plain or (with) cinnamon raisins] (got013), and a menu of the day including '*kōhī* or *kōcha*' [Coffee or black tea] (kom088). A similar practice is use of the ampersand, for instance in '*resutoran* & *shoppu*' [Restaurants & shops] (osa038; see Loveday, 1996: 137), or a plus symbol, as in '*higawari pasuta* + *dorinku bā*' [Pasta of the day + drink bar] (meg033). Enumerations can be concluded with the term 'etc.', as in '*richōkagu chūgokukagu* etc' [Old-style Korean furniture, Chinese furniture, etc.] (sbu075).

The examples are listed in Table 5.29. The table closes with a case of code- and script-mixing on the syntactic level. It is a sticker displaying the slogan 'STOP *za poi*'. Attached to a lamp-post in Nishinippori (nis042), the sticker is an appeal not to litter. The slogan contains the English word 'stop' and the definite article 'the', which becomes *za* in Katakana

**Table 5.29** Examples of lexical and syntactic code- and script-mixing

| Survey number | Text on sign | English paraphrase |
|---|---|---|
| meg033 | 内容はSTAFF まで | For contents see staff |
| osa057 | 雨の日 10%off | On rainy days 10% off |
| sbu080 | ステキなDESSERT SET | Lovely dessert set |
| har022 | ライス or パン | Rice or bread |
| got013 | プレーンor シナモンレーズン | Plain or (with) cinnamon raisins |
| kom088 | コーヒー or 紅茶付 | With coffee or black tea |
| osa038 | レストラン&ショップ | Restaurants & shops |
| meg033 | 日替りパスタ＋ドリンクバー | Pasta of the day + drink bar |
| sbu075 | 李朝家具　中国家具 etc | Old-style Korean furniture, Chinese furniture, etc. |
| nis042 | STOP ザ・ポイ | Stop littering |

transliteration. The term *poi* is an onomatopoetic expression denoting the act of throwing something away. The degree of mixing in this slogan, concerning both language and script, is extremely high and, due to the ambiguous nature of the *za* as mediator between the rather English-looking 'STOP' and the Japanese *poi*, very smoothly organised. A clear classification of the sentence as either Japanese or English is problematic. Even if one considers both the 'STOP' and the *za* to have already become part of Japanese, the syntax is still that of an English imperative clause. To speakers of English, on the other hand, the slogan remains incomprehensible without sufficient proficiency in Japanese.

Code- and script-mixing do not only affect lexicon and syntax but may reach down to the morphological level. Thus we find several instances of word formation coalescing Kanji & Kana with the Roman alphabet. Examples such as 'COFFEE & RESTAURANT *jonasan*' (ugu033), 'Mansion & Hotel *sezāru*' (meg032), and 'GAME *rasubegasu*' (sbu060) have already been mentioned in section 5.6. The data contain several other instances where morphemes of the two languages in their respective scripts are combined into common and even proper nouns. A PC department store in Akihabara (aki033), for instance, is called 'COMPUTER OFFICE*kan*' [-building, -hall] and a similar business in Takadanobaba (tak037) has written 'PC • OA*kan*' on its shop sign. Another example is 'BEER*zen*' [-dish, -meal], which was found on the sign of a pub in Okachimachi (oka044).

All these formations have in common that they combine one or several Roman alphabet elements on the left with a Kanji & Kana head on the right. It can also be the other way round. Three examples from the sample are a *'hashikatsu* BLDG.', the name of a building in Akihabara (aki046), a *'karaoke*ROOM' at a pub in Shinbashi (sin007), and a *'risaikuru*BOX' [recycle] outside a convenience store in Tamachi (tam021). Similar instances of code-mixing may happen without script-mixing. Thus, there is an Italian restaurant in Shibuya (sbu116) named 'Spaghetti-Ya' [-shop, -business]. Two examples where morphological patterns of English are represented in Japanese (Katakana) script were found in Meguro: *'menzu pāma'* [Men's perm] (meg002) and *'dezaināzu manshon'* [Designers' apartments] (meg008). A third example, already mentioned in section 5.7, is *'emuzu dansu akademī'* [M's Dance Academy] (sug032).

Finally, in one case at least, code- and script-mixing were apparently intended to affect the phonological level. A steak house in Shinagawa (sna043) with a bilingual menu attached outside offered a dish called 'Bloomin' Onion'. In order to import this term into the Japanese script without losing the stylistic implication of the missing <g> at the end of the gerund, the apostrophe was included, too, resulting in *'burūmin' onion'*. Hard to imagine, with regard to both graphemic and phonemic levels, what left-out entity the apostrophe is supposed to represent here.

The above examples show that code- and script-mixing are not confined to lexical issues but affect the whole system, including morphosyntax and even pseudo-phonemic matters. Table 5.30 gives the

**Table 5.30** Examples of morphological and pseudo-phonemic mixing

| Survey number | Text on sign | English paraphrase |
|---|---|---|
| ugu033 | COFFEE & RESTAURANT ジョナサン | Jonathan |
| meg032 | Mansion & Hotel セザール | César |
| sbu060 | Game ラスベガス | Las Vegas |
| aki033 | COMPUTER OFFICE 館 | -building |
| tak037 | PC • OA 館 | -building |
| oka044 | BEER 膳 | -dish |
| aki046 | 箸勝 BLDG. | Hashikatsu (proper name) |
| sin007 | カラオケ ROOM | Karaoke |
| tam021 | リサイクル BOX | Recycle |
| sbu116 | Spaghetti-ya | -shop |
| meg002 | メンズパーマ | Men's perm |
| meg008 | デザイナーズマンション | Designers' apartments |
| sug032 | エムズ・ダンスアカデミー | M's Dance Academy |
| sna043 | ブルーミン'オニオン | 'Bloomin' Onion' |

terms discussed in their original graphic representation. Many other examples are dealt with by Loveday (1996: 120–4), who has also designed a classificatory scale gauging the degree of graphic assimilation.

## Chinese and Korean

Tokyo's two other foreign languages, Chinese and Korean, are very different from each other with regard to graphic idiosyncrasies. The most remarkable point of the 62 signs of the sample containing Chinese texts is variation in script use. One generally distinguishes two basic types of character sets (_hànzì_) for writing Chinese. Simplified short characters are in use on the Chinese mainland, whereas Hong Kong and Taiwan have retained the older, non-simplified, characters. Matters get further complicated by the fact that Japanese Kanji, the set of characters used for writing Japanese, differs slightly from both systems. However, many characters are identical in shape for all three sets and therefore cannot be unambiguously identified when considered in isolation.

Most texts of the sample classified as Chinese are written in short-style characters. In total, Chinese texts containing only short-style characters and characters identical for all three sets were identified on 50 signs. In the same way, texts on another five items could be determined to be texts written in long-style characters. The residuary seven items are problematic because they display Chinese texts containing distinctive characters of more than one set: short-style and Japanese characters on a menu in Takadanobaba (tak040) and on a shop sign in Shin-Ōkubo (sok095); long-style and Japanese characters on a shop sign in Takadanobaba (tak061, tak062) and on menus in Harajuku (har054) and Hamamatsuchō (ham038); and long-style, short-style, and Japanese characters on a menu in Shinbashi (sin011).

Instances of script-mixing occur in both print (ham038, sin011, har054, sok095) and handwriting (tak040, tak061–062) but only on bottom-up signs. Official sign writers are more careful to keep apart the different types of character sets, though they produce both signs in short-style (e.g. uen004) and signs in long-style characters (e.g. sok040). The above observations are summarised in Table 5.31.

Mixing in Chinese texts also involves lexical issues. Two examples are given in Figures 5.20 and 5.21: a warning sign outside a bank in Shinbashi (sin039) and a sign at a stationery shop in Shin-Ōkubo (sok095). In the former case, the warning 'THE PLACE POLICE MEN PATROL' is available in Japanese, English, Chinese, and Arabic. It is concluded by a Japanese-only line about the originator of the sign, Atago Police Station. Idiosyncrasy with regard to the Chinese version arises out of the fact that the term for 'police officer' represented by the first three characters is a lexical import from Japanese. Though it will be understood by

**Table 5.31** Chinese texts on the signs of the sample

| Survey no. | Type of sign | Cases | Character set | | | TD vs. BU | Script quality |
|---|---|---|---|---|---|---|---|
| | | | Short-style | Long-style | J. Kanji | | |
| uen004 | Guidance | 1 | * | | | TD | Print |
| nis027 | Garbage info | 1 | * | | | TD | Print |
| kom050 | Bicycle warning | 1 | * | | | TD | Print |
| sug105-021 | Bicycle warning | 17 | * | | | TD | Print |
| ike025-027 | Bicycle warning | 3 | * | | | TD | Print |
| mio005-024 | Bicycle warning | 20 | * | | | TD | Print |
| sok030 | Bicycle warning | 1 | * | | | TD | Print |
| sbu004-009 | Warning | 6 | * | | | BU | Print |
| tak041 | Menu | 1 | | * | | BU | Print |
| sok040 | Guidance | 1 | | * | | TD | Print |
| osa059-060 | Shop sign | 2 | | * | | BU | Print |
| sin039 | Warning | 1 | | * | | BU | Print |
| tak040 | Menu | 1 | * | | * | BU | Hand |
| sok095 | Shop sign | 1 | * | | * | BU | Print |
| tak061-062 | Shop sign | 2 | | * | * | BU | Hand |
| har054 | Menu | 1 | | * | * | BU | Print |
| ham038 | Menu | 1 | | * | * | BU | Print |
| sin011 | Menu | 1 | * | * | * | BU | Print |

Notes: TD=Top-down, BU=bottom-up.

people with Chinese backgrounds, the term is not in common use in the Chinese-speaking world.

The shop sign in Shin-Ōkubo offers telephone cards for international calls. It contains three languages – from top to bottom, Korean, Japanese, and Chinese. Noteworthy about the Chinese version is that it combines both different character sets and different languages. It can be subdivided into three parts: (1) The first four characters, meaning 'international telephone', are Chinese short-style characters (though the first one is identical in shape to the equivalent Japanese Kanji), but the corresponding Japanese Kanji characters would have the same meaning; (2) the fourth and sixth characters could be either Chinese (long- or short-style) characters or Japanese Kanji, but the combination of the two characters in the meaning of 'discount' is common only in Japanese; and (3) the last two characters are Japanese Kanji meaning 'sale' (though the

**Figure 5.20** Warning sign at a bank (sin039)

**Figure 5.21** Sign offering international telephone cards (sok095)

last but one character could also be (long-style) Chinese), but the corresponding Chinese characters would have the same meaning. Taken in total, it is impossible to unambiguously classify the phrase as either Chinese or Japanese, though it appears most reasonable to consider it to be Japanese that is partially written in Chinese short-style characters. The example demonstrates the degree to which Japanese and Chinese writing may be intertwined.

Evidently, then, there is a considerable degree of Japanese–English and Japanese–Chinese contact. It comes as a surprise that no comparable mixing occurs in Korean texts on the signs of the sample. One possible explanation for the differences between English and Chinese on one hand and Korean on the other is that both English and Chinese are represented in scripts also used for writing Japanese: Roman alphabet and (genetically related though slightly differing) logographic character sets, respectively. Many of the interferences observed for the two languages may have been provoked by the contiguity of the writing systems in use. Comparable graphic interfaces with Korean no longer exist. The Korean language nowadays is mainly written in Hangul, a writing system that has no overlays with the Chinese or Roman script. This is not to say that code- and script-mixing between Japanese and Korean does not exist. Kim (2003), for instance, has identified a couple of such cases in a survey of the linguistic landscape of Osaka. However, a contiguous writing system appears to have a facilitating function in generating interferences and producing linguistic hybrids.

On a less theoretical level, the above differences can be interpreted with regard to the producers of the signs. We can assume that idiosyncrasies in foreign language use are indicative of a sign writer of Japanese origin. The Korean texts on the signs are likely written exclusively by people of Korean origin, while texts in English and Chinese frequently have a Japanese originator. This supports the assumption formulated in section 5.4 that the Korean population write their signs by and for themselves, whereas English and Chinese signs are provided mainly by Japanese agents. On the other hand, it should not be omitted that long-term residents of Chinese origin account for at least some of the instances of code- and script-mixing.

The basic finding of this section is that the signs of the sample manifest a high degree of language contact. This refers not only to the appearance and co-appearance of various languages and scripts as discussed in previous sections, but also to the way the languages and scripts affect each other internally. We have seen that many instances of idiosyncratic language use can be explained as resulting from interferences of orthography, morphosyntax, and lexicon. In extreme cases it is impossible to allocate a certain term or expression to one language. Such observations particularly hold true with regard to Japanese–English mixing, but to some extent apply to Japanese–Chinese blends, too. The fact that Korean texts on the signs of the sample remain virtually un-affected suggests that the use of contiguous writing systems is an important factor in facilitating linguistic interference.

## 5.10 Layering

One of the earliest motivations for conducting linguistic landscape research has been detecting ongoing changes in a city's linguistic outward appearance. This is ideally done in a 'real time' manner, that is, by conducting two or more successive surveys at different points in time and directly comparing the results. A methodologically sound example of this type of study is the series of empirical investigations by the Council of the French Language (CLF, 2000; see 3.2) in Montreal. Since this type of study demands a great amount of time and money, it is usually conducted by research institutions or other organisations rather than by individual researchers.

An alternative way of examining diachronic changes in the linguistic landscape when data from only one point in time are available is to concentrate on the coexistence of older and newer editions of a given sign. Some observations in this respect have been made in earlier research, too. An example is East Jerusalem, where older and newer versions of a tiled street sign allowed Spolsky and Cooper (1991: 5–8; see 3.3) to reconstruct recent changes in the city's linguistic landscape. Their conclusions were feasible despite the fact that only one point in time was considered. In diachronic linguistics this way of investigation is well known as 'apparent-time' studies. Though such approaches to language change have commonly been confined to spoken language, Spolsky and Cooper's example from Jerusalem demonstrates that an apparent-time study can be an appropriate method for investigations into written language as well.

The closing section of this chapter takes an apparent-time look at Tokyo's linguistic landscape. The coexistence of older and newer versions of a given type of sign will be referred to as 'layering' – a term used in diachronic linguistics to denote the concurrence of different meanings taken on by a linguistic form over time (Aitchison, 2001: 113–14). This phenomenon has been described by Hopper (1991: 22) in the following way: 'Within a broad functional domain, new layers are continually emerging. As this happens, the older layers are not necessarily discarded, but may remain to coexist with and interact with the newer layers.'

In a less metaphorical sense the term 'layering' has of late been used in linguistic landscape research. Scollon and Scollon (2003: 137; see 3.7) refer to it as a sign 'attached to another sign in such a way that one is clearly more recent and more temporary' because it is 'not part of the original semiotic design'. The present study adopts this terminology, if with a slightly different focus. Of interest is not how layering is intentionally used to convey a sense of newness, but rather, in a similar way to what Spolsky and Cooper were able to show, how layering lays bare different linguistic states in the recent history of the city. According to Wienold this phenomenon can be noticed

> when one inscription takes over the function of an older inscription of similar purpose. Thus, I found in London several instances of two street signs bearing the same street name, one right above the other. Rather than canceling the older inscription by replacing it with the newer one, the new one was placed next to it. This is not an uncommon phenomenon at all. (1994: 648–9)

Instances of layering can be examined with regard to four points, which I will discuss in turn: (1) number of languages and scripts contained; (2) amount of foreign language information; (3) occurrence of idiosyncrasies; and (4) proportion of languages and scripts. As in section 5.8, the examples include some monolingual versions of multilingual signs without which many instances of layering would go unnoticed. They were found inside the 28 survey areas but are not part of the sample.

## Number of languages and scripts

The most obvious development that the coexistence of older and newer signs visualises is an increase in number of languages and scripts. One example is street block signs, which used to be inscribed in Kanji & Kana only. An early review of internationalisation initiatives by the Metropolitan Government (TMG, 1992: 47–53) shows that the first Romanisation initiatives for these signs started in the late 1980s. The results of my survey suggest that more than a decade later this process has been considerably advanced but not completed. In Nishinippori, for instance, I found within a few metres both a newer sign with an additional Romanised line (nis021) and an older one not containing any transliterations (nis+01). They are given in Figures 5.22 and 5.23.

A similar co-occurrence was observed in Shibuya, where three of the new (sbu052–054) and two of the older types of signs (sbu+01 and sbu+02) had been set up. A fourth token of the older type was found in Yoyogi (yoy+01), the only area containing a non-Romanised street block sign without a co-appearing Romanised one. These four monolingual items face a total of 47 multilingual street block signs found in the survey areas. Thus, in quantitative terms, the newer version of the sign has come to dominate the linguistic landscape of the city today, though it has not yet completely supplanted the older ones.

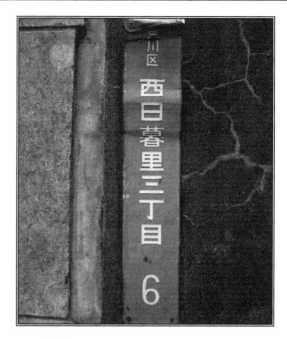

**Figure 5.22** Street block sign (nis+01)

**Figure 5.23** Street block sign (nis021)

Similar observations of this type of layering can be made for various other sorts of signs: monolingual area maps, information plates on traffic lights, and subway signs about train departures coexist with Japanese–English counterparts (nis+02 vs. ugu007, sok+01 vs. har057, kan+01 vs. har081, respectively); information plates on postboxes are available with and without Braille (e.g. sug142–144 vs. ike044–047); and Japanese-only information boards about garbage collection occur side by side with corresponding Japanese–English versions and, occasionally, even quatri-lingual editions in Japanese, English, Chinese, and Korean (aki+01 vs. aki113 vs. nis027). This latter type of sign will be discussed in more detail in the next subsection.

## Amount of foreign language information

The second type of layering refers to the amount of foreign language information. An example is the just-mentioned bilingual and quatri-lingual garbage collection signs. In Tokyo three types of garbage are regularly collected by the local garbage offices on different days of the week: combustibles, non-combustibles, and recyclables. Information boards are used to indicate the designated collection points and to explain what type of garbage is to be put out when. Three examples are given in Figures 5.24, 5.25, and 5.26.

The Japanese–English versions of the sign differ slightly with regard to the amount of English information. While in most cases all necessary directions are available in both languages (e.g. sin071; see Figure 5.25), there are bilingual versions of the sign that are not particularly helpful to people who know English but not Japanese. One example was found in Hamamatsuchō (ham065; see Figure 5.24). The sign indicates that this is a 'Recyclables and Waste Collection Point' and gives the days of the week when it is serviced, 'TUE' and 'FRY' (*sic*), 'SAT', and 'THU', respec-tively. This knowledge, however, is of little use because information about what type of garbage is collected on these days is available only in Japanese. This makes it impossible to observe the basic rules of garbage collection without at least some literacy in Japanese.

A similar problem applies to the quatrilingual version of the sign found in Nishinippori (nis027; see Figure 5.26). The high density of text on the sign shows that considerable effort was made to provide as much information as possible in all four languages. Five types of contents are available not only in English but in Chinese and Korean translation as well: 'Waste Collection Point'; 'No Parking'; the types of garbage; 'Please take out garbage . . .'; and 'System for making requests . . .'. Another two types of information are given in Japanese and English only. One is the two lines *denwa* and 'TEL' at the bottom of the sign, the other is the days of collection given to the right of the respective types of garbage.

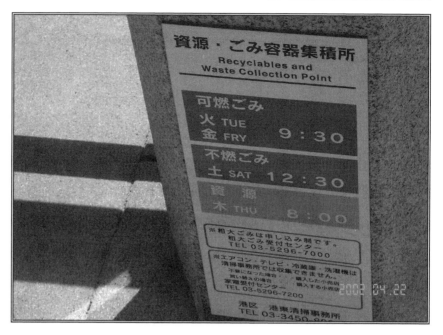

**Figure 5.24** Information board about garbage collection (ham065)

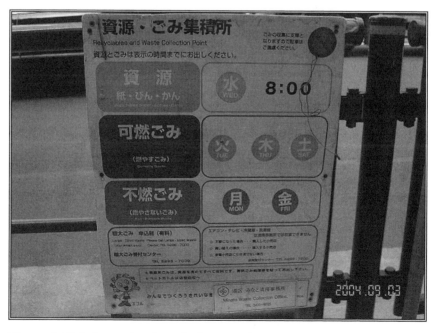

**Figure 5.25** Information board about garbage collection (sin071)

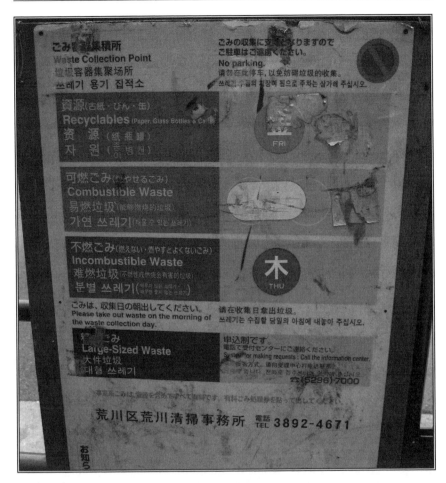

**Figure 5.26** Information board about garbage collection (nis027)

Lack of Chinese and Korean translation in this second case may be an impediment for Chinese and Korean residents in understanding what type of garbage is collected when, which is arguably the most essential information of the sign.

Although it is not likely that there are any sizeable numbers of Chinese or Korean residents in Nishinippori who won't be able to make sense of the sign, the three examples show that there is a hierarchy in the amount of information to be provided. In this hierarchy, Japanese is on top, English is in second position, and Chinese and Korean follow in rank. Assuming that the three types of garbage collection signs have come into use in succeeding order, it becomes observable how a growing number of languages other than Japanese are charged with a growing amount of information content.

## Occurrence of idiosyncrasies

A look at older and newer versions of multilingual signs also suggests a decrease in linguistic idiosyncrasies, particularly with regard to the use of English. A few examples will illustrate this. Thus, the idiosyncratic use of the determiner in 'A Fire Extinguisher' on emergency signage in Yoyogi (yoy001) and Ebisu (ebi007) is absent on the newer types of fire extinguisher boxes set up in Ōsaki (osa071), Shinagawa (sna009), Tamachi (tam005), and Hamamatsuchō (ham004). Another example is older and newer postboxes. While an information plate on the older type indicates that the left-hand slot is reserved for ordinary 'LETTER POST-CARD', the corresponding plate on the newer one gives the two terms with plural inflections. In the 28 survey areas I came across a total of 15 postboxes, 10 of which were of the old type and five of the new one. This suggests that, as of 2003, the older type of postbox was still prevailing but the newer one was gaining ground.

Within the group of newer postboxes there is further variation in Japanese Braille and English. One of the four plates in Hamamatsuchō (ham047), unlike the corresponding plates on the four other new post-boxes, translates the Japanese term *renrakusaki* not as 'Where to contact', but gives the rather idiosyncratic phrase 'Where to make connect'. A similar observation can be made with regard to the use of Braille, which on the plate in Hamamatsuchō is a complete one-to-one mapping of the Japanese print version. As a result, the unusual term *shushū jikoku* [Collection times], whose meaning can hardly be understood unless written in Kanji, is directly transliterated into Braille. A comparable idiosyncrasy on another plate on the postbox in Hamamatsuchō (ham046) is the transliteration of the focus particle *wa*, which is given in the Braille version as *ha*. Though this is the orthodox representation of the morpheme in Kana script, in Braille the particle is usually given as *wa*. Since the corresponding plates on the four other new postboxes do not contain these idiosyncrasies, they must be improved versions that are younger than those found in Hamamatsuchō.

A third example is signs at traffic lights for pedestrians. Many pedestrian lights in Tokyo are set out of service during night hours or work only when a button down at the post is pushed. In most such cases an information plate has been installed near the button in order to tell passers-by to do so. As can be understood from a summarising report by the Metropolitan Government (TMG, 1989: 47), this plate into the late 1980s used to be monolingual Japanese. The first Japanese–English version of the sign, produced in 1988, contained the English text 'TO

CROSS STREET PUSH BUTTON AT NIGHT'. Though a minimum of pragmatic competence will enable most English-speaking persons to understand the intended meaning, the syntax of the sentence is slightly misleading. Therefore, an alternative version of the sign has recently come into use, this time with a wording less easy to be misunderstood: 'TO CROSS STREET AT NIGHT PUSH BUTTON'.

All three versions still occur in the streets of Tokyo. As the data of my survey suggest, however, the latest version is now clearly dominating. It made up 14 of the 22 items found in the survey areas. Six other items were bilingual signs of the earlier type, whereas only two items of the monolingual Japanese version were left over.

## Proportion of languages and scripts

The fourth type of layering concerns changes in the proportion of languages and scripts on signs. This point applies to most of the examples given so far, but the development in some cases is particularly striking. One example is stickers by security companies, which are a characteristic component of the linguistic landscape of Tokyo. Attached to the property to be protected, they abound on private and corporate buildings. They function both as deterrence to possible wrongdoers and as advertisements for the security companies.

One major security company is called *sōgō keibi hoshō*, which is Romanised on their website as 'SOHGO SECURITY SERVICES CO., LTD.'. More commonly, however, they used to refer to themselves by the alphabet acronym 'SOK', which represents the reading of the first (*sō*) and third (*kei*) characters of their official Japanese name. According to an e-mail inquiry at the company's public relations section in April 2003, the oldest version of their sticker found in the survey areas was one officially in use until 1992. It is given in Figure 5.27. The sticker contains the image of an eagle, which was the company's emblem at the time, and two lines of Japanese text underneath. The upper line names the service provided by the company, *sōgō gādo shisutemu* [Comprehensive guard systems]; the lower line gives its official Japanese name.

In 1992 a newer sticker in similar design came into use. It still contained the eagle emblem on top and the company's name at the bottom. However, as can be seen in Figure 5.28, the upper line has been replaced by the alphabet acronym 'SOK', which makes Roman letters gain a foothold on the sign. An even more remarkable change in the design of the sticker occurred in 1997. The version of the sticker that came in use then not only contains the alphabet acronym but also English text. The top line of the sign, which on the older versions of the sticker was occupied by the eagle emblem, now displays the phrase 'Security & Safety'. The middle part of the sticker is covered by an enlarged version of the

**Figure 5.27** Sticker of a security company (ugu+01)

**Figure 5.28** Sticker of a security company (ugu+02)

alphabet acronym, while the original Japanese name of the company appears at the bottom of the sign in a comparatively small font size only. The sticker is shown in Figure 5.29.

A look at the situation in the 28 survey areas reveals that the latest edition of the sticker has long since surpassed the older versions in frequency. The sample contains 38 items of the latest, bilingual, version of the sticker, two examples of the intermediate type, and another two of the oldest type. Thus, while the new sticker is now virtually omnipresent on the walls of the city, the older versions have become a rare sight. The coexistence of the three variants of the sign permits the observation not only of a general shift from monolingual to multilingual formats but of ongoing changes in proportions of languages and scripts as well.

On a supplementary note, the company changed their acronym once more briefly after the survey, in July 2003. Though their official Japanese name has remained as it used to be, the company since then have referred to themselves as 'ALSOK'. Consequently, the 1997 version of the sticker was replaced by a new one with the five-letter acronym. However, not only the acronym changed, but what the letters are supposed to stand for changed, too. According to a May 2003 press release by the company, the letters of the new term are to represent the following concepts: 'Amenity', 'Live', 'Security', 'Only 1', and 'Kindness' (ALSOK, 2003). The

**Figure 5.29** Sticker of a security company (ugu062)

letters that once used to abbreviate a Japanese term now are reinterpreted as referring to English terms. The script remains the same, but the language changed.

In general, the four types of layering discussed in this section suggest that Tokyo's linguistic landscape is undergoing major changes at the moment. These changes appear to be more easily observable for top-down than for bottom-up signs, though this would be hard to quantify. The direction of the changes is as follows: use of a higher number of languages and scripts; more information provision in languages other than Japanese; more consciousness of linguistic idiosyncrasies; and, partially as a result of the former points, more visual prominence of languages and scripts other than Japanese in the streets of the city.

# Chapter 6
# *Conclusions*

The chief aim of this book has been to show that the study of language on signs is a valuable research tool for exploring the coexistence of different languages and scripts, both in a society and in its individual parts. Having analysed the Tokyo sample of signs on the basis of nine categories, the basic question to be addressed now is what insights about linguistic diversity in the Japanese capital can be gained from this analysis. In other words, what do multilingual signs in Tokyo tell us about multilingualism in Tokyo? In order to formulate some concrete answers to this point, we will now come back to the three guiding questions formulated in Chapter 4. The closing section summarises these findings and sets them into a larger, non-Japan-specific context.

## 6.1 Linguistic Landscaping By Whom?

Who is responsible for the visibility of linguistic diversity in the streets of Tokyo? Section 5.4 has shown that the majority of multilingual signs have a non-official, bottom-up, background. However, a rate of top-down signs just below 30% reveals that official agencies clearly have their share in Tokyo's multilingual landscape, too. Combined with a brief look at recent guidelines about official sign writing, the results of the case study thus demonstrate how a certain part of Tokyo's multilingual landscape is consciously planned and enacted by the Metropolitan Government, the 23 wards, and other administrative agents.

Official and non-official signs exhibit essentially different characteristics with regard to the languages contained (5.2), their functions (5.6), and their visual prominence (5.7). Top-down signs use a limited number of languages – Japanese, English, and, to a smaller extent, Chinese and Korean – which in most cases constitute translations or transliterations of each other. Care is taken that Japanese appears as the prominent language. Bottom-up signs frequently deviate from these principles. They contain a greater variety of languages and use them in a functionally complementary way. Code preference on these signs is not necessarily given to Japanese.

Another important point concerning the producers of multilingual signs is the geographic distribution of languages other than Japanese within the city. The analysis in section 5.5 has shown how Tokyo's two major linguistic minority groups in certain parts of the city have started to visually make their presence felt. The appearance of Chinese and Korean on signs in the western and north-western parts of the Yamanote Line loop is a novel component of Tokyo's linguistic landscape that reflects its growing linguistic diversity. However, whereas Chinese signs predominantly have an official background, the majority of signs in Korean are written by the Korean population themselves.

Differences between indexical and symbolic use of foreign languages by foreign and non-foreign sign writers have been identified when discussing patterns of code preference in section 5.7. I have dealt with this point only in a rather cursory way because it involves some problems. Though the semiotic distinction between the two types of language use is of theoretical value, it is difficult to apply in practice because both functions are often enacted simultaneously. True, Japanese is the default language for signs of Japanese origin, and consequently Japanese in a prominent position is the unmarked case. However, interpreting all Japanese-owned signs with English in a prominent position as instances of symbolic language use would be misjudging the role of English in Japan. English has become an indispensable part of the Japanese language itself. It may be used as a symbol for 'something which is not present or which is ideal or metaphorical' (Scollon & Scollon, 2003: 133), but recurrent use of the symbol at the same time indexes common language preference patterns within Japanese society. As English is becoming part of Japanese, the symbol itself is becoming an index. I have made no attempt to quantify the distinction between indexical and symbolic language use in my survey, because it is unreasonable to clearly separate the one from the other.

A methodological shortcoming of the survey is the lack of qualitative data about the monolingual signs contained in the 28 areas, of which we know little more than that they must have been there. This makes it difficult to evaluate in any meaningful way the relationship between display language and commercial domain, a point frequently discussed in previous research. An analysis of language use and business type is feasible only when control data about monolingual signs are available. For instance, in the absence of data on monolingual signs of hairdressers and beauty parlours, no conclusions about the seemingly high frequency of English on multilingual shop signs of this type of business are warranted. In retrospect, it would appear reasonable to work with a smaller number of signs but include all items irrespective of their linguistic properties.

## 6.2 Linguistic Landscaping For Whom?

With regard to the target group of multilingual signs I have introduced the analytical category 'part writing' (5.6) based on which I have formulated the following rule of thumb: multilingual signs providing translations or transliterations were produced with a non-Japanese readership in mind; multilingual signs without translations or transliterations target the Japanese public. The fact that both types of signs are recognisable in quantitative terms proves that Tokyo's multilingual landscape is intended to serve the foreign as well as the Japanese population. To the former it makes available originally Japanese information in languages other than Japanese; to the latter it has become an indispensable ingredient of everyday communication.

The functional distribution of Japanese and English on Tokyo's signs allows for conclusions about the linguistic profile of the Japanese readership. Where no translation or transliteration is available, the use of English is confined to titles, slogans, business names, etc. Information of a more specific nature is reserved for the Japanese text. This pattern suggests that, although constantly confronted with signs containing English or English-looking elements, the average passer-by is not expected to understand more complex contents in English. On the other hand, the mere existence of a sizeable number of multilingual signs with simple English text given without a corresponding Japanese version implies that a minimal degree of proficiency in English has become a basic requirement in order to understand a Japanese sign these days. Instances of marked code preference suggest that the completely monolingual Japanese reader is an exception, as it were – a new linguistic minority group left behind by current developments.

A last point concerning the target group of multilingual signs refers to the way in which information in two or more languages is presented. As shown in section 5.8, the overwhelming majority of the signs display two or more texts in one frame. Their multilingual nature is revealed at first sight, while separate frames for different languages are rare. The one-frame-for-all-languages design is so common in Tokyo that in some cases apparently corresponding foreign versions of a Japanese text are added for the sole purpose of making a sign look less monolingual. This is indicative of the general demand by the Japanese public for signs with a visibly multilingual format. This finding is in line with the overall tendency of traditionally monolingual cities to desire multilingual signs, which has been identified in section 4.3. The Japanese host population's fondness for foreign languages, particularly English, is a factor no less important in shaping Tokyo's linguistic landscape than the growing presence of non-Japanese people in Japan.

## 6.3 Linguistic Landscape *Quo Vadis*?

Languages displayed on public signs in Tokyo do not merely coexist, but internally affect each other in various ways. As could be seen in section 5.9, this is most obvious with regard to Japanese and English. The texts on the signs of the sample provide many examples of both Japanese-influenced uses of English and English-influenced uses of Japanese, depending on which of the two functions as the matrix language. As a result, it is often impossible to unequivocally determine the language that is being used. Script choice is of only limited value here because, as we have seen, the Roman alphabet must be considered a common option for writing Japanese, too. In this respect, Suzuki (2002: 4–5, 144–9) has emphasised that what Japan faces at present is not the oft-quoted Katakana overflow, but in fact an overflow of Roman letters. A similar point has recently been made by Akizuki (2005: 181–3). To further complicate things, English loans are commonly integrated into Japanese text in their original English spelling ('Snack', 'Menu', 'Make') rather than in a Romanised version of the Japanese layer ('Sunakku', 'Menyū', 'Mēku'). This way of graphic representation, which has been referred to as 'rewriting' (see 5.9), produces hybrid terms impossible to clearly assign to one language.

As to the two other foreign languages of Tokyo, it could be observed that instances of interference are more frequent for Chinese than for Korean. This suggests that the use of a contiguous writing system facilitates internal language contact. The occurrence of Japanese–Chinese hybrids in the linguistic landscape of present-day Tokyo in some sense is reminiscent of the early days of writing in Japan. Seeley (1991: 25–39) has identified many comparable instances of mixing on script monuments of the 6th and 7th centuries CE, when Chinese characters had first been introduced to Japan. Referred to by Seeley as 'hybrid style texts', they follow the conventions of literary Chinese but to some extent are linguistically influenced by Japanese. The fact that some 1500 years later we still find similar cases on signs in central Tokyo indicates that Japanese writing itself is a form of coagulated language contact.

More recent developments in Tokyo's linguistic landscape have been recaptured by comparing older and newer versions of a given type of sign. As discussed in the closing section of Chapter 5, this approach reveals changes of language usage patterns in favour of languages and scripts other than Japanese in the streets of the city. One may see here initial indications of a changing linguistic self-perception in Japanese society, particularly when considering that many of the changes are the results of deliberate language-planning activities by official agencies. That it is not only the state and its organs that account for the presence of foreign languages and scripts in Tokyo's linguistic landscape is best exemplified by the high frequency of Korean signs in Shin-Ōkubo, where we witness first instances of a non-Japanese population taking possession of the linguistic landscape.

On the other hand, it should not be forgotten that around 80% of the signs found in the survey areas are monolingual Japanese signs. Examining multilingualism in Tokyo by reading the signs thus reveals that Tokyo is a city that still predominantly functions in one language. No other language apart from Japanese can be assumed to be generally used and understood in everyday life; no other language – not even English – is likely to threaten the dominance of Japanese in the nearer future. In this sense, Tokyo is not a multilingual city. Nevertheless, a look at the linguistic landscape reveals various indications of a city's growing linguistic diversification – signs of multilingualism in Tokyo.

## 6.4 Back to the Start

The city is a place of language contact, as we have said, and the signs in public space are the most visible reminder of this. The linguistic landscape not only tells you in an instant where on earth you are and what languages you are supposed to know, but it contains information going far beyond this. It provides a unique perspective on the coexistence and competition of different languages and their scripts, and how they interact and interfere with each other in a given place.

In closing let us briefly recapture the basic plan of this book. We began by discussing the semiotic background to language on signs. We have dealt with terminological issues concerning the linguistic landscape and delineated what this type of research should and should not include. The next chapter has given a comprehensive overview of linguistic landscape research worldwide. It could be demonstrated that previous approaches have much in common, different research environments and sometimes highly differing research interests notwithstanding. These common points have provided the basis of the framework put forward in this book. Based on three research questions and nine analytical categories, it has been intended to serve as a first blueprint for the systematic analysis of linguistic landscape data.

The applicability of the framework has been tested by analysing a sample of 2444 multilingual signs in Tokyo. The results show that the visibility of languages and scripts other than Japanese in the streets of the city is a product of three main factors:

(1) official language policies aiming at an 'internationalisation' of Tokyo;
(2) a growing share of non-Japanese residents in some parts of the city;
(3) favourable attitudes towards the visibility of foreign languages, particularly English, on the part of the Japanese host population.

Thus we see how both Japanese and non-Japanese actors are involved in the making of Tokyo's multilingual landscape: Japanese produce multilingual signs for non-Japanese (factor 1); non-Japanese produce multilingual signs for non-Japanese (factor 2); and Japanese produce multilingual signs for Japanese (factor 3).

The total of Tokyo's linguistic landscape can be read as reflecting ongoing changes in the Japanese language regime (Coulmas & Heinrich, 2005). It can be seen that the country's much-quoted monolingualism is about to lose relevance in a globalising world. The uncontested role of Japanese as the national language and its ideological underpinning as the essence of being Japanese now increasingly face pressure, both from above and below. On the one hand, Japan's monolingual worldview is challenged by the power of English as the default language for all sorts of international communication (factor 1) and as the most prestigious foreign language domestically (factor 3). On the other hand, a look at Tokyo's linguistic landscape also demonstrates that a growing number of people with non-Japanese backgrounds have started making their languages heard and seen (factor 2).

All in all, the present study suggests that much can be learned from linguistic landscape research, particularly when qualitative and quantitative issues are dealt with in combination. In this respect the vital importance of a sound methodology for collecting and analysing linguistic landscape data must be re-emphasised. It is highly desirable that a set of standard tools be developed to become generally accepted and further refined in the years to come. Ideally, this would allow one day for directly comparing linguistic landscape studies from different environments to each other. Identifying some of the universals and local differences in sign writing and reading worldwide would have much to contribute to multilingualism and language contact research, as well as the study of language and society as a whole. There is still a long way to go, but, as some of the latest approaches discussed in Chapter 3 suggest, first important steps in this direction have now been taken. The present study has been intended to contribute to this development.

# Appendix: The 28 Survey Areas

| Area name | Ward | Street blocks | Street name | Traffic light numbers* |
|-----------|------|---------------|-------------|------------------------|
| Tōkyō | Chiyoda | Marunouchi 1, 2 | | 101–52/53 101–33 |
| Kanda | Chiyoda | Kanda-kajichō 3 | Chūō dōri | 103–04•33•46 103–36 |
| Akihabara | Chiyoda | Soto-kanda 1, 3 | Kanda-myōjin-dōri | 103–17 103–19 |
| Okachimachi | Taitō | Ueno 3, 4 | Kasuga-dōri | 660–22 660–21 |
| Ueno | Taitō | Ueno-kōen | | 660–53 660–71 |
| Uguisudani | Taitō | Ueno-sakuragi 1, 2 | Kototoi-dōri | 661–63 661–46 |
| Nishinippori | Arakawa | Nishinippori 3, 4 | Dōkan-yama-dōri | 666–42 666–14 |
| Tabata | Kita | Tabata 1 | | 552–26 552–10 |
| Komagome | Bunkyō Toshima | Hon-komagome 6 Komagome 1 | Hongō-dōri | 548–14 548–39 |
| Sugamo | Toshima | Sugamo 1 | Hakusan-dōri | 593–13 594–33 |
| Ōtsuka | Toshima | Minami-ōtsuka 2, 3 | | 549–18 549–67 |
| Ikebukuro | Toshima | Minami-ikebukuro 1 | | 550–24 550–40 |
| Mejiro | Toshima | Mejiro 1, 2 | Mejiro-dōri | 551–36 551–91 |
| Takadanobaba | Shinjuku | Takadanobaba 3 | Waseda-dōri | 437–35•03 437–40 |

147

**Appendix** The 28 survey areas *continued*

| Area name | Ward | Street blocks | Street name | Traffic light numbers* |
|---|---|---|---|---|
| Shin-Ōkubo | Shinjuku | Ōkubo 1, 2 | Ōkubo-dōri | 436–39 436–95 |
| Shinjuku | Shinjuku | Shinjuku 3 | Shinjuku-dōri | 436–02 436–02 |
| Yoyogi | Shibuya | Sentagaya 5 | Meiji-dōri | 332–08 332–35 |
| Harajuku | Shibuya | Jingūmae 1, 6 | Omotesandō | 332–45 332–01H |
| Shibuya | Shibuya | Shibuya 1, 2 | Miyamasu-zaka | 331–02 331–84 |
| Ebisu | Shibuya | Ebisu 11, 12 | | 331–91 331–38 |
| Meguro | Shinagawa | Kami-ōsaki 3 | Meguro-dōri | 217–06•14•49 217–36 |
| Gotanda | Shinagawa | Higashi-gotanda 1, 2 | 217–35 | 217–15 |
| Ōsaki | Shinagawa | Ōsaki 1 | Yamate-dōri | 217–24 217–37 |
| Shinagawa | Minato | Takanawa 3, 4 | | 110–01 110–44 |
| Tamachi | Minato | Shiba 5 | | 109–02 109–15 |
| Hamamatsuchō | Minato | Hamamatsuchō 1, 2 | | 108–47 108–01 |
| Shinbashi | Minato | Shinbashi 6 | Sotobori-dōri | 108–02 108–15 |
| Yūrakuchō | Chiyoda | Yūrakuchō 1 | Harumi-dōri | 101–08BCD 101–812KLMN |

*Note*: *Traffic lights in Tokyo are designated by five-digit numbers written on a box attached to one of the poles. Note that the pole with the box may be positioned outside the actual survey area.

# References

Aitchison, J. (2001) *Language Change: Progress or Decay?* (3rd edn). Cambridge: Cambridge University Press.

Akizuki, K. (2005) *Arienai nihongo* [*Impossible Japanese*]. Tokyo: Chikuma Shobō.

ALSOK (Sōgō keibi hoshō kabushiki gaisha) (2003) *Puresu rirīsu: shin kōporēto burando ni tsuite no oshirase* [*Press Release: About Our New Corporate Brand*]. On WWW at http://www.alsok.co.jp/news/press2003/ci030527.html.

Backhaus, P. (2004) Uchi naru kokusaika: Tōkyōto no gengo sābisu [Internal internationalisation: The City of Tokyo's language services]. In T. Kawahara (ed.) *Jichitai no gengo sābisu* [*Language Services of Local Governments*] (pp. 37–53). Yokohama: Shumpusha.

Baetens Beardsmore, H. (2000) Bruxelles. In W.F. Mackey (ed.) *Espaces urbains et coexistence des langues* (*Terminogramme* 93–4) (pp. 85–102). Quebec: Office de la langue française.

Bagna, C. and Barni, M. (2005) Dai dati statistici ai dati geolinguistici: Per una mappatura del nuovo plurilinguismo. *SILTA* (*Studi Italiani di Linguistica Teorica e Applicata*) 34 (2), 329–55.

Bagna, C. and Barni, M. (2006) Per una mappatura dei repertori linguistici urbani: nuovi strumenti e metodologie. (In preparation.)

Ben-Rafael, E., Shohamy, E., Amara, M.H., and Trumper-Hecht, N. (2001) *Linguistic Landscape and Multiculturalism: A Jewish-Arab Comparative Study* (Final report). Tel Aviv: The Tami Steinmetz Center for Peace Research.

Ben-Rafael, E., Shohamy, E., Amara, M.H., and Trumper-Hecht, N. (2004) *Linguistic Landscape and Multiculturalism: A Jewish–Arab Comparative Study*. Tel Aviv: Tami Steinmetz Center for Peace Research.

Ben-Rafael, E., Shohamy, E., Amara, M.H., and Trumper-Hecht, N. (2006) Linguistic landscape as symbolic construction of the public space: The case of Israel. *International Journal of Multilingualism* 3 (1), 7–30.

Bouchard, P. (2000) Montréal. In W.F. Mackey (ed.) *Espaces urbains et coexistence des langues* (*Terminogramme* 93–4) (pp. 31–57). Quebec: Office de la langue française.

Calvet, L.-J. (1990) Des mots sur les murs: Une comparaison entre Paris et Dakar. In R. Chaudenson (ed.) *Des langues et des villes* (*Actes du colloque international à Dakar, du 15 au 17 décembre 1990*) (pp. 73–83). Paris: Agence de coopération culturelle et technique.

Calvet, L.-J. (1993) *La sociolinguistique*. Paris: Presses universitaires de France.

Calvet, L.-J. (1994) *Les voix de la ville: Introduction à la sociolinguistique urbaine*. Paris: Payot et Rivages.

Carroll, T. (2001) *Language Planning and Language Change in Japan*. Richmond: Curzon.

Cenoz, J. and Gurter, D. (2006) Linguistic landscape and minority languages. *International Journal of Multilingualism* 3 (1), 67–80.

Chandler, D. (2002) *Semiotics: The Basics*. London: Routledge.

CLF (Conseil de la langue française) (2000) *La langue de l'affichage à Montréal de 1997 à 1999*. Quebec: Conseil de la langue française.

Comune di Roma (2005) I numeri di Roma (No. 1, 2005). Rome: Commune di Roma, Ufficio di Statistica. On WWW at http://www.comune.roma.it/was/repository/ContentManagement/information/P1648114312/1563_numero1_05.pdf.

Coulmas, F. (1996) *The Blackwell Encyclopedia of Writing Systems*. Oxford: Blackwell.

Coulmas, F. (1999) Metaschrift. In J. Wertheimer and S. Göße (eds) *Zeichen lesen Lese-Zeichen* (pp. 31–54). Tübingen: Stauffenburg.

Coulmas, F. (2003) *Writing Systems: An Introduction to Their Linguistic Analysis*. Cambridge: Cambridge University Press.

Coulmas, F. (2005) *Sociolinguistics: The Study of Speakers' Choices*. Cambridge: Cambridge University Press.

Coulmas, F. and Heinrich, P. (eds) (2005) Changing language regimes in globalizing environments: Japan and Europe. *International Journal of the Sociology of Language* 175/176.

Crawford, J. (ed.) (1992) *Language Loyalties: A Sourcebook on the Official English Controversy*. Chicago, IL: University of Chicago Press.

Daoust, D. (1990) A decade of language planning in Québec: A sociopolitical overview. In B. Weinstein (ed.) *Language Policy and Political Development* (pp. 108–30). Norwood, NJ: Ablex.

Denoon, D., Hudson, M., McCormack, G., and Morris-Suzuki, T. (eds) (1996) *Multicultural Japan: Palaeolithic to Postmodern*. Cambridge and New York: Cambridge University Press.

Douglass, M. and Roberts, G.S. (eds) (2000) *Japan and Global Migration: Foreign Workers and the Advent of a Multicultural Society*. London and New York: Routledge.

Dumas, G. (2002) Québec's language policy: Perceptions and realities. In J. Baker (ed.) *Language Policy: Lessons from Global Models* (pp. 152–63). Monterey, CA: Monterey Institute of International Studies.

Evens, B. (ed.) (2000) *The World's Stupidest Signs*. London: O'Mara.

Extra, G. and Yağmur, K. (eds) (2004) *Urban Multilingualism in Europe: Immigrant Minority Languages at Home and at School*. Clevedon: Multilingual Matters.

García, O. and Fishman, J.A. (eds) (1997) *The Multilingual Apple: Languages in New York City*. Berlin: Mouton de Gruyter.

Goebel Noguchi, M. and Fotos, S. (eds) (2001) *Studies in Japanese Bilingualism*. Clevedon: Multilingual Matters.

Gorter, D. (2006) Introduction: The study of the linguistic landscape as a new approach to multilingualism. *International Journal of Multilingualism* 3 (1), 1–6.

Gottlieb, N. (1995) *Kanji Politics: Language Policy and Japanese Script*. London and New York: Kegan Paul International.

Griffin, J.L. (2004) The presence of written English on the streets of Rome. *English Today* 20 (2), 3–7 and 47.

Günther, H. and Pompino-Marschall, B. (1996) Basale Aspekte der Produktion und Perzeption mündlicher und schriftlicher Äußerungen. In H. Günther and

O. Ludwig (eds) *Schrift und Schriftlichkeit/Writing and Its Use* (Vol. 2) (pp. 903–17). Berlin and New York: de Gruyter.

Haarmann, H. (1989) *Symbolic Values of Foreign Language Use: From the Japanese Case to a General Sociolinguistic Perspective*. Berlin: Mouton de Gruyter.

Halliday, M.A.K. (1978) *Language as Social Semiotic*. London: Edward Arnold.

Hannahs, S.J. (1989) Bilingual advertising in a region of linguistic conflict: Some Belgian approaches. In P. Nelde (ed.) *Urban Language Conflict (Plurilingua VII)* (pp. 57–63). Bonn: Dümmler.

Harweg, R. (1979) Dauer-Deixis oder Wie sind Beschriftungen zu lesen? *Orbis* 28, 5–26.

✕ Hirose, K. (2005) Tenji [Braille]. In S. Shinji and H. Shōji (eds) *Jiten Nihon no tagengo shakai* [*Dictionary of Japan's Multilingual Society*] (pp. 152–5). Tokyo: Iwanami.

✓ Honna, N. (1995) English in Japanese society: Language within language. In J.C. Maher and K. Yashiro (eds) *Multilingual Japan* (pp. 45–62). Clevedon: Multilingual Matters.

Hopper, P.J. (1991) On some principles of grammaticization. In E.C. Traugott and B. Heine (eds) *Approaches to Grammaticalization* (Vol. 1) (pp. 17–35). Amsterdam: Benjamins.

Horvat, A. (2000) *Japanese Beyond Words: How to Walk and Talk Like a Native Speaker*. Berkeley, CA: Stone Bridge Press.

Huebner, T. (2006) Bangkok's linguistic landscapes: Environmental print, codemixing and language change. *International Journal of Multilingualism* 3 (1), 31–51.

Inoue, F. (1997) Market value of languages in Japan. *Nihongo kagaku* 2, 40–60.

Inoue, F. (2000) *Nihongo no nedan* [*The Price of Japanese*]. Tokyo: Taishūkan.

Inoue, F. (2001) *Nihongo wa ikinokoreruka* [*Will Japanese Survive?*]. Tokyo: PHP Shinsho.

Itagi, N.H. and Singh, S.K. (eds) (2002a) *Linguistic Landscaping in India with Particular Reference to the New States: Proceedings of a Seminar*. Mysore: Central Institute of Indian Languages and Mahatma Gandhi International Hindi University.

Itagi, N.H. and Singh, S.K. (2002b) Introduction. In N.H. Itagi and S.K. Singh (eds) *Linguistic Landscaping in India with Particular Reference to the New States: Proceedings of a Seminar* (pp. ix–xii). Mysore: Central Institute of Indian Languages and Mahatma Gandhi International Hindi University.

Jerome, J. (ed.) (1997) '*Please Take Advantage of the Chambermaid' and Other Silly Signs*. London: O'Mara.

Jewitt, C. and Oyama, R. (2001) Visual meaning: A social semiotic approach. In T. van Leeuwen and C. Jewitt (eds) *Handbook of Visual Analysis* (pp. 134–56). London: Sage Publications.

Joseph, J.E., Love, N., and Taylor, T.J. (2001) *Landmarks in Linguistic Thought II: The Western Tradition in the Twentieth Century*. London and New York: Routledge.

Keller, R. (1995) *Zeichentheorie*. Tübingen and Basel: Francke.

Kim, M. (2003) Gengo keikan kara mita Nihon no taminzokuka [Japan's growing ethnic heterogeneity seen from the linguistic landscape]. In H. Shōji (ed.) *Kokusai imin no jizon senryaku to toransunashonaru nettowāku no bunka jinruigaku* [*Cultural-ethnological Research on International Immigrants' Strategies of Independent Existence and Transnational Networks*] (pp. 175–90). Osaka: National Museum of Ethnology.

Kim, M. (2004) Nihon shakai to no kyōsei mezasu shinrai kankokujin [Newcomer South-Koreans heading for symbiosis with Japanese society]. In National Museum of Ethnology (ed.) *Taminzoku Nihon: zainichi gaikokujin no kurashi* [*Multiethnic Japan: Life and History of Immigrants*] (pp. 75–9). Osaka: Senri Foundation.

Kjørup, S. (2004) Pictograms. In R. Posner (ed.) *Semiotik/Semiotics* (Vol. 4) (pp. 3504–10). Berlin: de Gruyter.

Kress, G. and van Leeuwen, T. (1996) *Reading Images: The Grammar of Visual Design*. London: Routledge.

Labov, W. (1972) *Sociolinguistic Patterns*. Oxford: Blackwell.

Landry, R. and Bourhis, R.Y. (1997) Linguistic landscape and ethnolinguistic vitality. *Journal of Language and Social Psychology* 16 (1), 23–49.

Larsen, S. (1993) *Japlish: Photographs by Sally Larsen*. San Francisco, CA: Pomegranate Artbooks.

Lee, Y. (1996) *Kokugo to iu shisō: kindai Nihon no gengo ninshiki* [*The Kokugo Ideology: Language Awareness in Modern Japan*]. Tokyo: Iwanami.

Levine, M.V. (1990) *The Reconquest of Montreal*. Philadelphia, PA: Temple University Press.

Lie, J. (2001) *Multiethnic Japan*. Cambridge, MA: Harvard University Press.

Loveday, L. (1996) *Language Contact in Japan: A Sociolinguistic History*. Oxford: Clarendon Press.

Lützeler, R. (2002) Ausländische Zuwanderer in Japan. *Geographische Rundschau* 54 (6), 12–17.

MacGregor, L. (2003) The language of shop signs in Tokyo. *English Today* 19 (1), 18–23.

Machimura, T. (2000) Local settlement patterns of foreign workers in Greater Tokyo. In M. Douglass and G.S. Roberts (eds) *Japan and Global Migration: Foreign Workers and the Advent of a Multicultural Society* (pp. 176–95). London and New York: Routledge.

Mackey, W.F. (ed.) (2000) *Espaces urbains et coexistence des langues* (*Terminogramme* 93–4). Quebec: Office de la langue française.

Maher, J.C. and Yashiro, K. (eds) (1995) *Multilingual Japan*. Clevedon: Multilingual Matters.

Masai, Y. (1972) *Tōkyō no seikatsu chizu* [*Living Map of Tokyo*]. Tokyo: Jiji Tsūshinsha.

McArthur, T. (2000) Interanto: The global language of signs. *English Today* 16 (1), 33–43.

Milroy, L. (1980) *Language and Social Networks*. Oxford: Blackwell.

Mohan, S. (2002) Linguistic landscape and social identity: A case of Jharkhand. In N.H. Itagi and S.K. Singh (eds) *Linguistic Landscaping in India with Particular Reference to the New States: Proceedings of a Seminar* (pp. 230–40). Mysore: Central Institute of Indian Languages and Mahatma Gandhi International Hindi University.

Monnier, D. (1989) *Langue d'accueil et langue de service dans les commerces à Montréal*. Quebec: Conseil de la langue française.

Okuda, M. (1994) Joshō: nyūkamāzu (shinki kyojūsha) toshite no ajiakei gaikokujin chōsa oboegaki [Foreword: Memorandum of a survey about newcomer Asian foreigners]. In M. Okuda, Y. Hirota, and J. Tajima (eds) *Gaikokujin kyojūsha to nihon no chiiki shakai* [*Foreign Residents and Japan's Local Communities*] (pp. 11–35). Tokyo: Akashi Shoten.

Reh, M. (2004) Multilingual writing: A reader-oriented typology – with examples from Lira Municipality (Uganda). *International Journal of the Sociology of Language* 170, 1–41.

Rosenbaum, Y., Nadel, E., Cooper, R.L., and Fishman, J.A. (1977) English on Keren Kayemet Street. In J.A. Fishman, R.L. Cooper, and A.W. Conrad (eds) *The Spread of English* (pp. 179–96). Rowley, MA: Newbury House.

Ross, N. (1997) Signs of international English. *English Today* 13 (2), 29–33.

Saint-Jacques, B. (1987) Bilingualism in daily life: The Roman alphabet in the Japanese writing system. *Visible Language* 21 (1), 88–105.

Saussure, F. de (1916) *Course in General Linguistics* (C. Bally, A. Sechehaye, and A. Riedlinger (eds); W. Baskin, English trans., 1966). London: McGraw-Hill.

Schlick, M. (2002) The English of shop signs in Europe. *English Today* 19 (1), 3–17.

Scollon, R. and Scollon, S.W. (2003) *Discourses in Place: Language in the Material World*. London and New York: Routledge.

Seeley, C. (1991) *A History of Writing in Japan*. Leiden: Brill.

Shibatani, M. (1990) *The Languages of Japan*. Cambridge and New York: Cambridge University Press.

Singh, U.N. (2002) Linguistic landscaping: An overview. In N.H. Itagi and S.K. Singh (eds) *Linguistic Landscaping in India with Particular Reference to the New States: Proceedings of a Seminar* (pp. 7–19). Mysore: Central Institute of Indian Languages and Mahatma Gandhi International Hindi University.

Smalley, W.A. (1994) *Linguistic Diversity and National Unity: Language Ecology in Thailand*. Chicago, IL: University of Chicago Press.

Soanes, C. and Stevenson, A. (eds) (2003) *Oxford Dictionary of English* (2nd edn). Oxford: Oxford University Press.

Someya, H. (2002) Kanban no moji hyōki [Writing on signs]. In Y. Tobita and T. Satō (eds) *Gendai nihongo kōza dai 6 kan: moji hyōki* [*Modern Japanese Course Vol. 6: Letters and Writing*] (pp. 221–43). Tokyo: Meijishoin.

Spolsky, B. (1997) Multilingualism in Israel. *Annual Review of Applied Linguistics* 17, 138–50.

Spolsky, B. and Cooper, R.L. (1983) The languages of Jerusalem: Arab–Jewish relations in the Old City. Research report to the Ford Foundation, Bar-Ilan University.

Spolsky, B. and Cooper, R.L. (1991) *The Languages of Jerusalem*. Oxford: Clarendon Press.

Spolsky, B. and Shohamy, E. (1999) *The Languages of Israel: Policy, Ideology and Practice*. Clevedon: Multilingual Matters.

Stalph, J. (1996) Das japanische Schriftsystem. In H. Günther and O. Ludwig (eds) *Schrift und Schriftlichkeit/Writing and Its Use* (Vol. 2) (pp. 1413–27). Berlin and New York: de Gruyter.

Stanlaw, J. (2004) *Japanese English: Language and Culture Contact*. Hong Kong: Hong Kong University Press.

Stewart, P. and Fawcett, R. (2004) Shop signs in some small towns in modern Portugal. *English Today* 20 (1), 56–8.

Suzuki, Y. (2002) *Nihongo no dekinai nihonjin* [*Japanese Who Cannot Speak Japanese*]. Tokyo: Chuo Koron.

SWET (Society of Writers, Editors and Translators) (1989) *Japan Style Sheet: The SWET Guide for Writers, Editors and Translators*. Berkeley, CA: Stone Bridge Press (revised edition, 1998).

Tajima, J. (1994) Daitoshi innā eria ni okeru gaikokujin kyojū [Residence of foreigners in the inner areas of big cities]. In M. Okuda, Y. Hirota, and J. Tajima (eds) Gaikokujin kyojūsha to Nihon no chiiki shakai [Foreign Residents and Japan's Local Communities] (pp. 36–128). Tokyo: Akashi Shoten.

Takashi, K. (1992) Language and desired identity in contemporary Japan. Journal of Asian Pacific Communication 3 (1), 133–44.

Tanaka, S. (2000) Tōkyō no kokusai seisaku to gengo sābisu [Internationalisation policies and language services in Tokyo]. In T. Kawahara (ed.) Nihon no chihō jichitai ni okeru gengo sābisu ni kansuru kenkyū [Research into Language Services of Japanese Local Governments] (pp. 18–25). Tokyo: Japan Association of College English Teachers, Language Policy Special Interest Group.

Tōshikyō (Tōkyō shiryoku shōgaisha no seikatsu to kenri o mamoru kai) (1994) Shikaku shōgaisha machizukuri ankēto chōsa [Survey about visually disabled persons and city making]. Unpublished document, Tōshikyō.

Tōshikyō (Tōkyō shiryoku shōgaisha no seikatsu to kenri o mamoru kai) (2000) Yamanote sen kaidan tesuri tenji hyōji tenken chōsa hōkoku [Report about a survey of Braille signs at the handrails of the stairs in Yamanote Line stations]. Unpublished document, Tōshikyō.

Trudgill, P. (1974) The Social Differentiation of English in Norwich. London: Cambridge University Press.

Tsujimura, N. (1996) An Introduction to Japanese Linguistics. Oxford: Blackwell.

Tulp, S.M. (1978) Reklame en tweetaligheid: Een onderzoek naar de geografische verspreiding van franstalige en nederlandstalige affiches in Brussel. Taal en sociale integratie 1, 261–88.

Twine, N. (1991) Language and the Modern State: The Reform of Written Japanese. London: Routledge.

Waley, P. (2000) Tokyo: Familiarity and difference. In P. Marcuse and R. van Kempen (eds) Globalizing Cities: A New Spatial Order? (pp. 127–57). Oxford: Blackwell.

Wenzel, V. (1996) Reclame en tweetaligheid in Brussel: Een empirisch onderzoek naar de spreiding van Nederlandstalige en Franstalige affiches. In Vrije Universiteit Brussel (ed.) Brusselse thema's 3 (pp. 45–74). Brussels: Vrije Universiteit.

Wienold, G. (1994) Inscriptions in daily life. In A. Sabban and C. Schmitt (eds) Der sprachliche Alltag. Linguistik – Rhetorik – Literaturwissenschaft: Festschrift für Wolf Dieter Stempel (pp. 635–52). Tübingen: Niemeyer.

Wienold, G. (1995) Inschrift und Ornament oder Die Entfärbung der Objekte: Englische Inschriften in der japanischen Kultur der Gegenwart. Tübingen: Stauffenburg.

Witte, E. and Baetens Beardsmore, H. (eds) (1987) The Interdisciplinary Study of Urban Bilingualism in Brussels. Clevedon: Multilingual Matters.

Yonehara, R. (1997) Tōkyōto: tayōsei ni michita shimin shakai [Tokyo: Civil society full of diversity]. In H. Komai and I. Watado (eds) Jichitai no gaikokujin seisaku [Policies Towards Foreigners by Local Administrations] (pp. 129–53). Tokyo: Akashi Shoten.

Official Sources

MIC (Ministry of Internal Affairs and Communications) (2004) Dai 50 kai Nihon tōkei nenran [Japan Statistical Yearbook 2005]. Tokyo: Ministry of Internal Affairs and Communications.

MLIT/EcoMo (Ministry of Land, Infrastructure and Transport/EcoMo Foundation) (2001) Kōkyō kōtsū kikan ryokyaku shisetsu no idō enkatsuka seibi gaidorain [Guidelines to Improve Barrier-free Access to Public Transport Passenger Facilities]. Tokyo: EcoMo Foundation.

MLIT/EcoMo (Ministry of Land, Infrastructure and Transport/EcoMo Foundation) (2002) *Kōkyō kōtsū kikan ryokyaku shisetsu no sain shisutemu gaidobukku* [*Sign System Guidebook for Public Transport Passenger Facilities*]. Tokyo: Taisei Shuppan.

MLIT/JICE (Ministry of Land, Infrastructure and Transport/Japan Institute of Construction Engineering) (2003) *Dōro no idō enkatsuka seibi gaidorain* [*Guidelines for Smooth Movement in the Streets*]. Tokyo: Taisei Shuppan.

Shinagawa Ward (1994) Shinagawaku machi no sain kihon manyuaru [Shinagawa Ward basic manual about street signs]. Unpublished document, Shinagawa Ward Office, Tokyo.

TMG (Tokyo Metropolitan Government) (1989) *Kokusaika ni kansuru kakukyoku no torikumi jōkyō* [*The State of each Bureau's Internationalisation Measures*]. Tokyo: Tokyo Metropolitan Government, Bureau of Citizens and Cultural Affairs.

TMG (Tokyo Metropolitan Government) (1991) *Tōkyōto kōteki sain manyuaru (an)* [*Tokyo Manual about Official Signs* (Draft)]. Tokyo: Tokyo Metropolitan Government, Information Liaison Council.

TMG (Tokyo Metropolitan Government) (1992) *Tōkyōto kushichōson ni okeru kokusaika: jigyōtō ni kansuru chōsa kekka* [*The Internationalisation of Tokyo's Wards, Cities and Towns: Report about Running Projects*]. Tokyo: Tokyo Metropolitan Government, Bureau of Citizens and Cultural Affairs.

TMG (Tokyo Metropolitan Government) (1997) Ryokyaku annai hyōshiki setchi manyuaru [Manual about passenger guidance signage]. Unpublished document, Tokyo Metropolitan Government, Bureau of Transportation.

TMG (Tokyo Metropolitan Government) (2002) *Tosei yōran heisei 14 nenban* [*Handbook of the Metropolitan Government 2002*]. Tokyo: Tokyo Metropolitan Government, Metropolitan Assembly Bureau.

TMG (Tokyo Metropolitan Government) (2003) Gaikokujin ni mo wakariyasui machi no hyōki ni kansuru gaido [Guide for Making City Writing Easy to Understand Also to Foreigners]. Tokyo Metropolitan Government, Bureau of Citizens and Cultural Affairs. On WWW at http://www.seikatubunka.metro. tokyo.jp/index3files/gaikokujinhyouki.pdf.

TMG (Tokyo Metropolitan Government) (2004a) *Tokyo: City Profile and Government*. Tokyo: Tokyo Metropolitan Government, Headquarters of the Governor.

TMG (Tokyo Metropolitan Government) (2004b) *Jinkō no ugoki (heisei 15 nen chū) no gaiyō* [*Outline of Population Trends (As of 2003)*]. Tokyo: Tokyo Metropolitan Government, Bureau of General Affairs.

TMG (Tokyo Metropolitan Government) (2004c) *Gaikokujin tōroku jinkō: heisei 16 nen* [*Registered Foreign Population 2004*]. Tokyo Metropolitan Government, Bureau of General Affairs. On WWW at http://www.toukei.metro.tokyo. jp/gaikoku/ga-index.htm.

TMG (Tokyo Metropolitan Government) (2004d) *Jūmin kihon daichō ni yoru Tōkyōto no setai to jinkō* [*Households and Population According to the Basic Register of Residents*]. Tokyo: Tokyo Metropolitan Government, Bureau of General Affairs.

# *Index*